Vintage Fabrics

Identification & Value Guide

Judith Scoggin Gridley, Joan Reed Kiplinger
& Jessie Gridley McClure

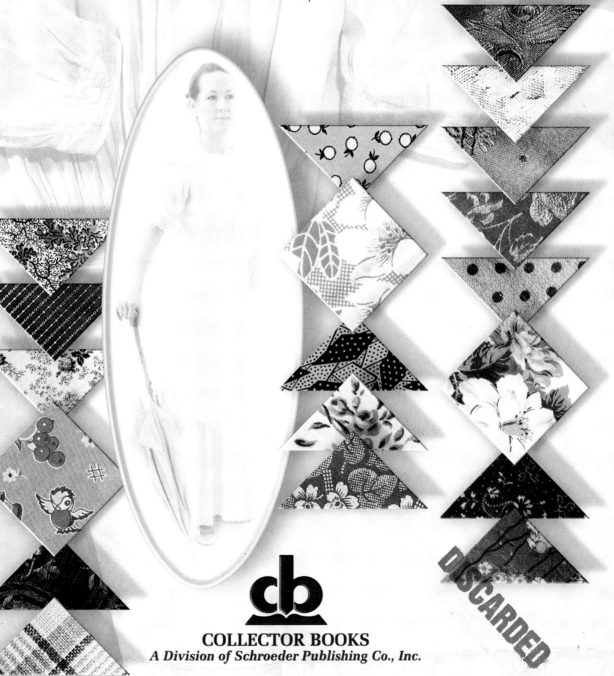

cb
COLLECTOR BOOKS
A Division of Schroeder Publishing Co., Inc.

Cover design: Beth Summers

Book design: Kelly Dowdy

Cover Photo: Charles R. Lynch

Artist: Jessie Gridley (McClure), daughter of Judith Scoggin Gridley

COLLECTOR BOOKS
P.O. Box 3009
Paducah, Kentucky 42002-3009
www.collectorbooks.com

The current values in this book should be used only as a guide. They are not intended to set prices, which vary from one section of the country to another. Auction prices as well as dealer prices vary greatly and are affected by condition as well as demand. Neither the authors nor the publisher assumes responsibility for any losses that might be incurred as a result of consulting this guide.

Searching For A Publisher?

We are always looking for people knowledgeable within their fields. If you feel that there is a real need for a book on your collectible subject and have a large, comprehensive collection, contact Collector Books.

Contents

Acknowledgments 4

Preface 5
   Why We Collect Vintage Fabric 6

Fabrics on Parade 7
   Cotton and Linen 7
   Nylon 90
   Rayon and Acetate 92
   Silk 95
   Wool 107

Buying, Pricing, and Thread Count 115
   What to Look for and What to Avoid 115
   The Importance of Thread Count 120

Fabric Identification by Fiber, Weave, and Appearance .121
   Fabric Identification by Fiber and Burn Test 121
   Fabric Identification by Weave Structure 125
   Fabric Identification by Appearance: The Look-alikes 128

Fabric Identification by Width, Brand Names, Finishes, and Mills 132
   Common Widths, 1880s – 1959 132
   Common Brand Names of Fabrics and Finishes 136
   Popular Brand Name Finishes 140
   Common Vintage Man-Made Brand Names 141
   Prominent Vintage Textile Mills, Converters, and Manufacturers 143
   Textiles — A Woven Part of American History 152

Bibliography 157

Acknowledgments

It takes many persons to produce a book. Our thanks to those who first suggested and supported the idea about a guide to old fabrics per se, and to the following who shared their patience, knowledge, talents and collections to make this effort possible.

For technical textile and research assistance – Mary Humphries, textile author, for advisory assistance on gauze/leno, lappet and swivel weaves and textile terminology; and Linda Learn, Joan Mahone, Sheila Ramsey, and Betty Wilson for research assistance.

For photography assistance — James Cummings; David Fibush; Judy Grow; Mary Ann Kennedy, Linda Learn; Sue Reich; and the staff at Super Color Photo Lab, Spokane WA : Jennifer Baker, Brandon Bertolucci, Nikki Johnson, and Kyle Smith.

For manufacturer, company, and association archival information, photographs, and advertisements — Mary K. Jensen, assistant to the director, American Sheep Industry Association Inc.; George W. Shuster, president and CEO, and Barbara Gray, Cranston Print Works Company™; Barbara Pandos, U.S. DuPont brand manager, E.I. Du Pont de Nemours and Company; Roy Bowen III, president, and Liz Hopkins, Georgia Textile Manufacturers Association; Stephan Logan, Indigo® Instruments; Pauline Delli-Carpini, Masters of Linen; T. Cotton Nelson, public relations manager, National Cotton Council of America; Arlene May and Nancy Turk, Archival Section, Sears, Roebuck & Co.; Ted Matthews, corporate vice president communications, Springs Industries; Ann Evans, historian, The White Homestead, Springs Industries; Peter Scotese, retired CEO and Board member Springs Industries and Chairman Emeritus Fashion Institute of Technology; Mary Connell, retired administrative assistant, Springs Industries; Pat DeSantis, Wm E. Wright Co.

For museum archival information and photographs — Bonnie Sousa, registrar, American Textile History Museum, Lowell MA; and Susan Barefoot, Old Mill Village Museum, New Milford, PA.

For textile brandnames, mills and manufacturer's records and printed literature – the Thelma Bernard publication collection; the late Pauline Bulawa collection of early man-made fibers and information; Charlotte Bull for The American Printing Company publication; the James Cummings collection for Boott and Stark Mills photos; the Shirley McElderry label, publication and periodical collection; the Pat L. Nickols publications collection; the Randy Rayfield collection for Springmaid ads; the Walter Stock collection for Helwig Silk Dyeing Co. information and photos; Terri Toretto, Rights and Permissions, Dover Publications Inc. for early textile woodcuts; the Betty Wilson catalog collection and Kimberly Wulfert for M.C.D. Bordon & Sons information.

For nineteenth and early twentieth century clothing, quilt and specialty fabric/feedsack collections -- Dana Balsamo, Laurette Carroll, Mary Connell, Xenia Cord, Pat Cummings, Dawna Ellenberger, Leigh Fellner, Judi Fibush, Barb Garrett, Judith Scoggin Gridley, Judy Grow, Mary Ann Kennedy, Dolores Lambert, Linda Learn, Shirley McElderry, the late Jesey Belle McGuire, Lillian Menzies, Mary Jane Poley, Sheila Ramsey, the late Emma Cattani Reed, Sue Reich, the late Audrey McGinnis Scoggin, Jane Clark Stapel, Sharon Stark and Bill Bascomb, and Betty Wilson.

For making this book a reality: The staff at Collector Books — editors Gail Ashburn, Carol Horman; assistant editor Amy Sullivan; cover designers Charles R. Lynch and Beth Summers; book designer Kelly Dowdy.

Preface

"A bit of cloth, whether it be woolen or cotton, linen, or silk, is one of the most interesting evidences of man's climb from days of savagery to twentieth century civilization."
- *The Story of Textiles*, Perry Walton, 1912

The perfect or ideal fabric reference book most likely will never be written; the logistics are too overwhelming in an industry that is a maze of complexities. Such a Herculean effort would be similar to the photographer who went mad trying to get a closeup of the horizon.

Fortunately there are many excellent books devoted to textiles on the market today, each capturing specific sectors of the textile world: textile science, printing and dyeing, fabric glossaries, vintage garments, dating by fabric color, quilting fabrics, and history of fabrics from vintage garments and other woven textiles, for example. They all offer information necessary to the study of textiles.

The purpose of this book is to fill a void (as far as we are aware) in information geared to vintage fabrics as a loom product, as yardage, and as a desirable product in today's marketplace. We chose the 1880s – 1959 period due to greater selection of reasonably priced fabrics currently accessible on the marketplace. The decision to include the 1950s was necessary as this was a transitional decade which gave birth to first and second generations of synthetics yet still remained a dominant stronghold for traditional, natural fiber fabrics.

Vintage Fabrics is intended as a quick reference that will benefit textile collectors in all fields with the purchasing and identifying of vintage cloth — novices, seamstresses, costumers and re-enactors, researchers, dealers, students, teachers, quilters, and those who simply like fabrics.

Fabric information in charts, glossaries, and photos is extended to include a wider range of cotton, silks, and wools plus early rayons and nylons, with their specific names, which are not featured in most general books on old fabrics. Further identification aids are provided by enlarged views of fabric surfaces, brand names, manufacturers, and information about how to distinguish between look-alikes.

Today, vintage is a word that seems to have no official beginning or end. It has become one of those all-encompassing terms which conveys old, depending on one's perspective of time and conception of old.

At one time a word most notably relegated exclusively to wine or crops, vintage made its generic buzzword appearance in the late 1970s, as fashion changed from "earth child" to "goddess glamour."

The craze was for styles from the 1920s through the 1940s, those vintage yesteryears as they were called.

Overnight, there were specialty magazines devoted to collecting anything vintage, with vintage inexplicably being extended back into time to mean anything from approximately around the turn of the century. Well, that's how the nostalgia game works.

With the passage of time, years were added to the other end of vintage, unfortunately pushing its time span to include the 1970s to early 1980s. It is most probable that as time goes on and the age range expands, vintage will become a meaningless word and need to be replaced.

Collecting vintage anything is probably today's foremost hobby. Dolls, toys, garments, cars, jewelry, textiles, Americana, Pez, mission furniture — name a topic and it's sure to be a hot collectible.

Many collectors are fortunate that there are official organizations which have strict age designations which pertain to their hobby. Dolls must be at least 75 years old to be called antique, 50 years or older to be collectible; modern for anything younger. Most other collecting categories fall under the method used for antique dating which requires an item to be 100 – 150 years or older to be called an antique.

For fabric collectors, there is no high official authority to establish a dating mechanism. Everyone determines what they think is vintage so that, in many instances, dealers are now conferring this favorite buzzword on cloth barely 15 – 20 years old. That is a big disappointment to buyers who envision something truly worthy of being given this distinction.

We believe there have to be timeframes to establish conformity so that when fabric collectors describe cloth as "vintage" or "old," it will be an implicitly understood term with a definite place in time. Perhaps eventually a consortium of textile associations, organizations, and museums will create a universal dating system to eliminate present confusion and frustration.

We hope the reader will find this book easy to use — the premise is to provide textile information in condensed and chart form, eliminating the need to wade through text.

It is our hope that the more this reference is used, the more the reader will become increasingly confident in understanding vintage fabric and be inspired to develop a keener knowledge through the reading of specialized textile books and old catalogs, advertisements, and magazines; and through the examination of fabrics, to become familiar with a fabric's name and characteristics.

Why We Collect Vintage Fabric

FOR BUSINESS

- resale
- costuming of all types
- crafts
- dating and appraising
- home decorating
- museum and other institutional display
- quilting
- re-enacting
- restoration and repair
- sewing clothes
- teaching
- textile history
- no particular reason; just can't help it

SPECIALIZED COLLECTIONS

- aprons
- collars and accessories
- doilies
- domestic linens
- feedsacks
- hankies
- hats
- purses and shoes
- military clothes and souvenirs
- needlework
- notions
- parlour pillows and fans
- period clothes for all ages
- quilts
- trims and laces

Fabrics on Parade

Descriptions are for American fabrics unless otherwise noted.

Featured in this illustrated section are many of the more common fabrics from the 1880s to 1959, and in some cases from earlier time periods, accompanied by enlarged views of their weave structures where feasible. Most of the names will be familiar to you, and all (except where indicated as presumably off-market) are still obtainable by their listed names. This section serves as a window to fabric selections of the times.

Definitions given are commensurate with this timeframe and may not reflect earlier or later descriptions for any given fabric. All brand name trademarks and registration symbols are automatically denoted by the capitalization of fabric names and finishes.

Accompanying photos of fabrics are fashions, labels, ads, and catalog illustrations showing how these fabrics were used for everyday use or as described by mills and manufacturers.

We hope this photo section, and information on brand names, mills, and manufacturers in "Fabric Identificaion by Appearance" will enable collectors to identify fabric names through photo comparison or by matching their fabrics' selvage markings, stampings, and labels to brand names listed here.

In keeping with the vintage concept, the term grey (var. gray), or grey goods, is used throughout this book for cloth just off the loom waiting to be converted cosmetically by bleaching, dyeing, printing, and specialty finishing. This word was used by mills, manufacturers, and textile educators and authors well into the 1950s and is, to some extent, still in use. Most of the textile industry today uses the word brown or unbleached goods or the French term, *greige*. Fashion circles prefer *greige*.

Note that much of the information presented here serves only as a starting point. The textile industry is complex with its numerous co-ventures and mergers, making it difficult to obtain origins and brand names of many fabrics. In addition, poor recordkeeping and damage from frequent fires have all but obliterated the archives in many of these mills and factories.

Our only regret is that actual swatches could not be provided, as there is nothing quite like touching and feeling the textures of fabric.

Cotton and Linen

Cotton, a vegetable or natural cellulosic plant fiber, is considered by the textile and fashion industries to be the most important and versatile fiber known in the world. While its origins have no accurate date, it is suspected that cotton has been in use since 8,000 years ago from bits of cloth and bolls found by scientists in Mexican caves. Recorded history reveals cotton being grown in India's Indus Valley and Egypt's Nile Valley as early as 3000 BCE. From there, cotton cultivation spread in all directions. It was the medieval Arab traders who called this fiber *quttan* or *kutn*, thus giving cotton its name. Today the world uses more cotton than any other fiber; it is the leading cash crop in the United States, a $24 billion industry, covering cotton fiber and cottonseed byproducts. See overview of linen in linen listing.

Alpaca

Plain weave. Originally wool or wool blends made to resemble and feel like hair of that animal. A perennial favorite in 1880s – 1890s for women's skirts and children's clothes By 1920 – 1930s it was a popular fabric of cotton warp with rayon filling or all rayon for lingerie, linings, blouses and accessories, commercial doll clothes, children's costumes, and found on many quilts of that era. A popular name for lower-grade alpaca was Halloween costume sleaze. Currently off-market by this name.

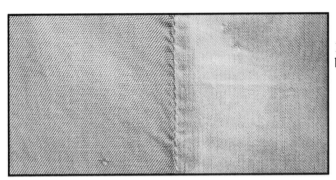

1930s alpaca with cotton warp, rayon filling is a backing from a doll's quilt.

Soldier blue, alpaca crepe two-piece dress suit, sequinned trimmed. *National Bellas Hess*, 1946 – 1947.

Barkcloth, Bark Crepe, Tapa Cloth

Also see osnaburg and cretonne. Plain or fancy weave. Originally a cloth made from bark of tapa trees in South Pacific. Modern name refers to cotton and rayon and other synthetics designed to resemble true barkcloth. It is used extensively for draperies, slipcovers, and other home furnishings. Osnaburg is the parent fabric in grey goods; cretonne is normally the fabric of choice in converted goods. Texture ranges from allover pebble to deep striations. Also called pebble cloth and pebble fabric. Seldom listed in most glossaries until the late 1940s – early 1950s; around 1920s the term referred to wool or silk with creped bark-like effect. By early 1950s, barkcloth was being hailed as the new texture sensation in catalogs such as *Montgomery Ward*. In 1954, *Spiegals* extolled a rayon/cotton version in Chromospun, Eastman's new rayon technological breakthrough rayon. Barkcloth was noted for its large floral or tropical cotton prints during 1930s – 1950s; as free-form designs in rayon and Fiberglass during late 1950s – 1960s; and in a novel departure, Elvis rock 'n' roll prints appeared in 1957!

1940s fancy dobby weave barkcloth. Also see "Fabric Identification by Fiber, Weave, and Appearance" on weave foundations.

One of barkcloth's many names, Birchbark; *Montgomery Ward*, 1942.

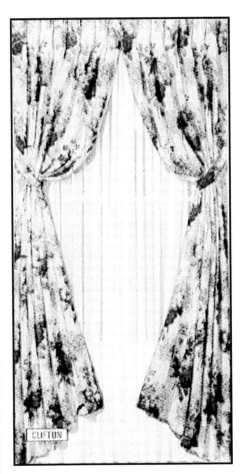

Precursor to the term barkcloth, these drapes were called pebble texture and were also available in cretonne. *Sears and Roebuck*, 1943. Courtesy Sears, Roebuck & Co.

Barkcloth's texture and strength make it serviceable for slipcovers. *Montgomery Ward*, 1957.

Basket Cloth

Any lightweight, soft, loosely woven cloth with pattern made in imitation of the appearance of baskets or in a smaller basket weave. See huguenot sacking, page 111. Other types of basket cloths are monk and druid.

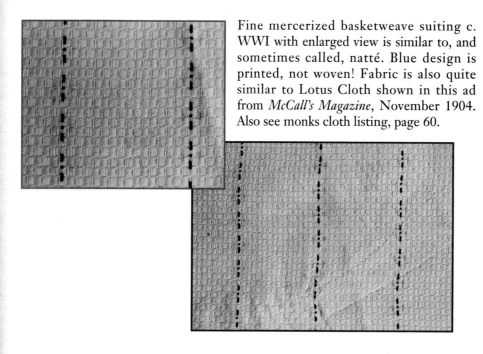

Fine mercerized basketweave suiting c. WWI with enlarged view is similar to, and sometimes called, natté. Blue design is printed, not woven! Fabric is also quite similar to Lotus Cloth shown in this ad from *McCall's Magazine*, November 1904. Also see monks cloth listing, page 60.

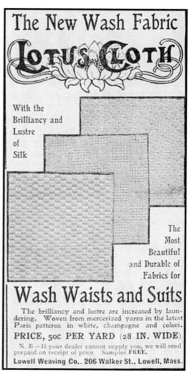

The New Wash Fabric
LOTUS CLOTH

With the Brilliancy and Lustre of Silk

The Most Beautiful and Durable of Fabrics for
Wash Waists and Suits

The brilliancy and lustre are increased by laundering. Woven from mercerized yarns in the latest Paris patterns in white, champagne and colors.

PRICE, 50c PER YARD (28 IN. WIDE)

N. B.—If your dealer cannot supply you, we will send prepaid on receipt of price. Samples FREE.

Lowell Weaving Co., 206 Walker St., Lowell, Mass.

Batiste

A linen created by Jean Batiste in thirteenth century Cambrai, France. A soft, fine, sheer, closely woven plain weave. Two-ply warp yarns give fabric a wavy appearance. Also made in wool, silk, rayon, and blends. It is lighter than (but similar to) challis, nun's veiling, & wool chiffon, and finer than nainsook. Part of lawn and mull family.

Early 1900s Holly brand fine, semi-sheer, printed batiste made by Arnold Print Works.

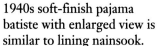

1940s soft-finish pajama batiste with enlarged view is similar to lining nainsook.

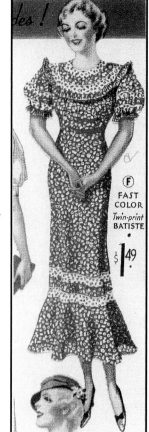

A frothy twin-print batiste frock for summer strolling. *Chicago Mail Order Co.* 1934.

Dress 5636

Delicate batiste for children's wear. *Pictorial Review*, May 1914.

Bedford Cord
See Piqué and Beford Cord (Cloth), page 70.

Bias Tape

The narrow fabrics field is so often overlooked as a source for cloth, yet this area has been an integral part of textile history and is a tale for another book. Beginning around the turn of the twentieth century and peaking in the 1950s, commercial bias tape as we know it, and other notions such as rickrack, were important trims for clothing and home accessories. They were available in every conceivable color, fiber, fabric, and design, and in a multitude of widths. More than 150 brand names have been documented so far with most entering and exiting during the 1920s – 1940s when bias tape was at the height of its popularity. As fashion and fibers changed from the 1950s onward, bias tape demand was affected, resulting in fewer fabrics and widths being produced. Modern choices are various grades of muslin or springy cotton/poly blends. Thanks to the revival of quilting, heirloom sewing, and crafting, bias tape is making a comeback to meet the sewing community's demands for variety and quality.

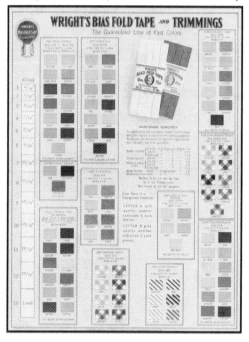  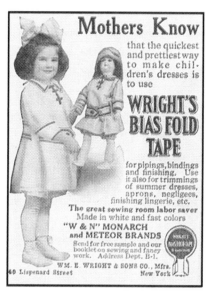

Bias tape and rickrack were important notions for trimming everything from clothes to household accessories. Wm. Wright & Sons led the way through its ads and booklets of extraordinary lithography. Bias tape chart, (1917 magazine ad) and bias trim ideas from booklet #21 (spring 1929) show the variety of fabrics and widths offered to home sewers for decorating with bias trims. Courtesy Wm. E. Wright Co.

Unusual bias tape brand names: Beauty, Cream of the Mills, Deco-Ric and Hope. Sheila Ramsey collection.

Broadcloth, Cotton (UK Poplin)

Closely woven plain weave, distinguished by random slubbing in filling yarns; not as prominent as its heavier weight relative, poplin. Slubbing barely visible when woven of fine quality or pima yarns. Use magnifying glass to detect and become familiar with this pattern as an aid to future identification. Cotton broadcloth (by that name) is thought to have come into being in the early 1920s, although its history dates back several centuries as a fine printed and fancy, or novelty, shirting fabric. In a medium weight it was popular in the 1940s – early 1950s for women's short-sleeve, two-piece summer casual suits and sometimes called dress poplin. Fabric mostly used for uniforms, shirts, blouses, casual wear, children's clothes, and is often found in quilts.

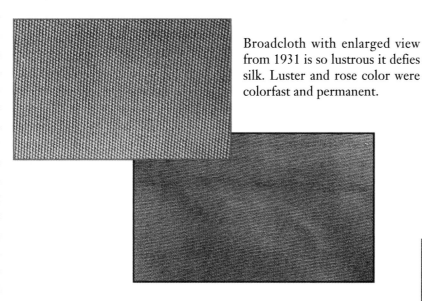

Broadcloth with enlarged view from 1931 is so lustrous it defies silk. Luster and rose color were colorfast and permanent.

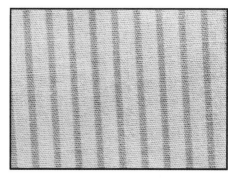

1950s broadcloth striped shirting suitable for quilting and casual wear.

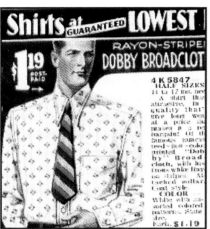

Men's fancy broadcloth shirt with a dobby weave. *Chicago Mail Order Co.* 1931.

"Hi Ho" broadcloth, the Lone Ranger rides again! *Montgomery Ward*, 1939 – 1940.

Broadcloth prints. *Montgomery Ward*, 1957.

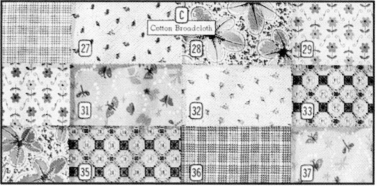

Calico (print)

Kalyko, mid-fourteenth century; name derived from Qualiqut or Calicut on the Malibar Coast in Calcutta, India and also known as Collicuthia, Med. Latin; Calecut and Qualecut, Port.; and Calicot, Fr. which is today's English pronunciation. First made as a sheer, fine gauze and coveted by nobility. Plain weave muslin; weave also known as calico weave to about 1900. American calico differs – many early printed calicoes before 1850s were woven of coarser yarns and were printed in two colors, usually a dark ground and a light color flower or design. Around 1880s colorful prints began appearing; yarn could be of finer grade, but this was limited. Some fabrics were oil-boiled for color fastness well into the first quarter of the twentieth century. Calico in the 1890s was described as a printed cloth coarser than muslin, used principally for inexpensive dresses such as shirtwaists, wrappers, etc. They were printed in two colors, one for ground and one for figure. After WWI calico print fabric was gradually replaced by percale, then by fine-quality plain wovens and dress muslin. Also see fine plain dress cottons in this section, page 32.

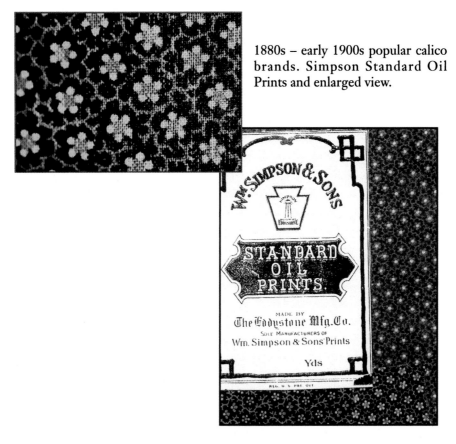

1880s – early 1900s popular calico brands. Simpson Standard Oil Prints and enlarged view.

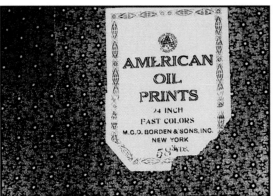

Borden's American Oil Prints for color fastness.

A Simpson ad in a June 1891 *Ladies Home Journal* proclaims the best in calico with a delaine finish (wool texture). Shirley McElderry collection.

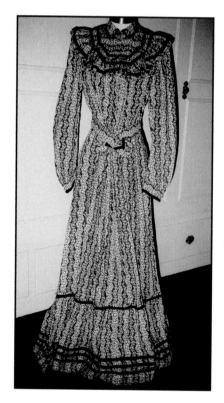

1890s calico morning wrapper. Mary Ann Kennedy collection.

Colorful 1890s Pennsylvanian German pillowcase with side opening. Barbara Garrett collection.

Cambric

Plain weave made in Cambrai, France. Has celebrated history as a multi-purpose fabric since fifteenth century. Made first of linen, then linen/cotton, then fine cotton or muslin by 1890s – early 1900. Cloth steadily declined in popularity since the early 1920s, although it is still available. Noted for its hard, smooth glossy surface and dense weave in dress goods and somewhat lineny texture; little or no sizing, highly glazed and polished on right side. Many other fabrics such as percale are given a cambric finish and sometimes listed as cambrics in 1920s – 1930s catalogs. Lining cambric is coarser, narrow, stiff, sized and glazed, does not launder, and is similar to paper cambric. Part of batiste, lawn, jaconet nainsook, mull, longcloth family.

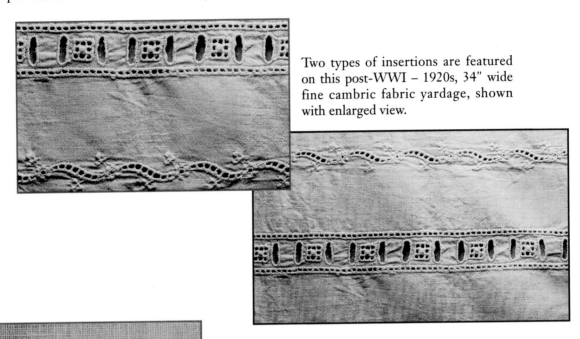

Two types of insertions are featured on this post-WWI – 1920s, 34" wide fine cambric fabric yardage, shown with enlarged view.

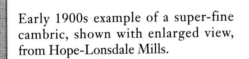

Early 1900s example of a super-fine cambric, shown with enlarged view, from Hope-Lonsdale Mills.

WWII offgrain cambric with kid (soft sheen) finish. Finish disappears after initial washing, leaving fabric limp and meshy. Good for crafts and costumes.

Cambric was an ideal fabric for nightwear, (*Peterson's Magazine* 1863), for trimming (J&J Cash frilling ad, *Ladies Home Journal*, November 1895), for undergarments (*Bellas Hess*, 1909), and for typewriter ribbon (*Sears & Roebuck Co.* 1943), courtesy Sears, Roebuck & Co. Also see cambric in longcloth listing, page 59.

Challie Chalinet, Challis, Challise, Challys, Shalli

From Anglo-Indian *shalee*, lightweight plain weave made from soft-spun cotton yarns or wool, or wool/cotton mixture, single warp, double filling. First manufactured in Norwich, England, 1832. It is usually a fabric of small floral prints and somewhat similar to voile in sheerness. In late 1870s – 1890s wool challis was referred to as a type of delaine, a collective term for wool. See mousseline delaine under wool page 108. Modern challis found in chain fabric stores and ready to wear, is mostly rayon.

1890s – early 1900s gauzy linen-texture challis print with enlarged view by M.C.D. Borden & Sons. Shirley McElderry collection.

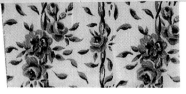

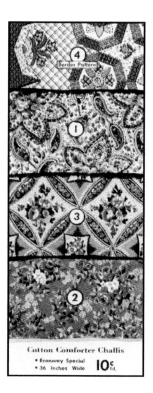

Cotton challis for making quilts and comforters. *Montgomery Ward* 1939 – 1940.

Chambray, Plain Weave

Another name derived from Cambrai, France. A type of gingham, characterized by dyed warp and white filling yarns. Usually striped or solid color, sometimes combined with piqué ribbing or with embroidered designs. Chambray was originally the fabric choice for the workingman's blue shirt, hence the term blue-collar worker.

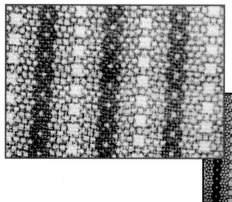

1890s – early 1900s Washington fast-color chambray with enlarged view by S.H. Greene & Sons Corp. Unusual as fabric is lightly glazed and design is printed, not woven — features not usually found in chambray.

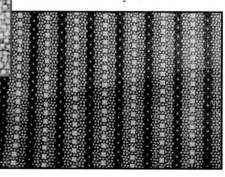

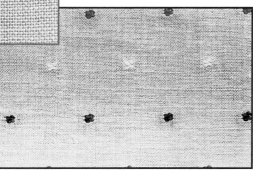

Fine chambray with enlarged view from 1931 with an embroidered dotted Swiss design created by box loom.

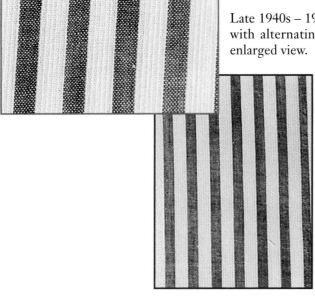

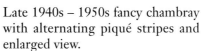

Late 1940s – 1950s fancy chambray with alternating piqué stripes and enlarged view.

1950s iridescent chambray was very trendy for all types of wear. Only enlarged view is shown to better capture coloring of fabric.

The famous blue-collar chambray work shirt. *Montgomery Ward,* 1925.

Chambray in casual mother and daughter styles. *Sears & Roebuck,* 1920. Courtesy Sears, Roebuck & Co.

Cheviot, Plain Weave

Woven, two-ply, twisted filling, and warp yarns; similar to and can be mistaken for utility gingham but is heavier. A popular shirting fabric of 1880s – 1890s. Named derived from Cheviot sheep as fabric is better known as a woolen.

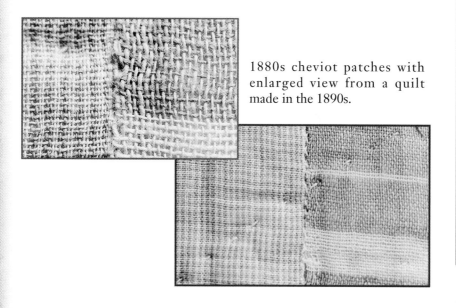

1880s cheviot patches with enlarged view from a quilt made in the 1890s.

Cheviot shirting for dresses and shirts. *Sears & Roebuck*, 1920. Courtesy Sears, Roebuck & Co.

Chintz and Glazed Chintz, Plain or Twill Weave

From Hindu *cheita* or Sanskrit *citra* meaning spotted, variegated or colored; or from Asian-Indian *chint* (pl. chintes) meaning fabric, name given to a kind of stained or painted calico produced in India. China is also credited with developing a type of similar hand-painted fabric. Earlier chintz from 1600 meant any lavishly printed fabric and was used interchangeably with glazed or unglazed calico. By 1850 chintz also referred to a glazed cotton printed with large polychrome designs of flowers and blossoming branches. In the 1880s – 1990s catalogs such as *Sears & Roebuck* and *Montgomery Ward* offered unglazed chintz under the name of English chintz. By 1920s, unglazed chintz fabric referred to drapery fabric of small gay figures, usually cretonne. Glazed chintz referred to closely woven fabrics, other than cretonne, which had a paraffin and calendered finish. Good grades can be washed. Ironing with wax paper helps to restore luster. Also see osnaburg, page 67, and cretonne, page 24.

Chintzes with glazing still intact from 1820s (l) with enlarged view and from 1840s.

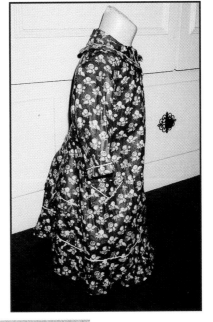

1880s girl's chintz print dress. Mary Ann Kennedy collection.

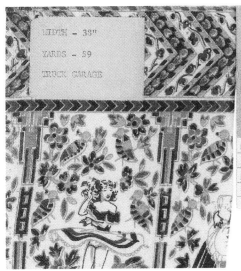

Springmaid chintz glazed by the Everglaze process, late 1940s – 1950s. Courtesy White Homestead Archives/Springs Industries.

Quilted chintz bedroom ensemble in harlequin pattern. *Montgomery Ward,* 1951.

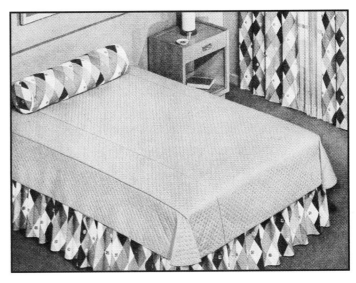

Cotton Crepe
See kimono crepe, page 52, and plissé, page 74.

Cottsey-Woolsey
Twill weave; cotton warp, wool filling of coarse yarns, extremely rough and scratchy; resembles tweed. Warp usually white or blue with filling in many colors. Thought to be same as, or similar to, linsey woolsey with cotton being used for linen. Most likely used for outer wear; definitely not a fabric to be next to skin. Nicknamed "cottsey-whatsy??" by collectors. Also see linsey-woolsey, page 58.

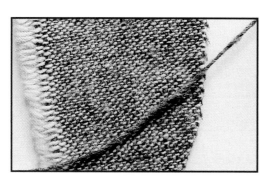

1830s fine-woven twill, white cotton warp, brown wool filling. Thought to be woven on commercial linen hand loom from Oley Valley, PA. Sharon Stark and Bill Bascom collection.

Coutil
French for drill, a warp-face herringbone twill heavier than jean. Cotton or cotton rayon blend, sometimes with figure or stripe effects. Dates back to eighteenth century. Mainstay for corsets and foundations, draperies, linings, and mattress coverings.

Front and back views of an early 1900s – WWI miniature coutil corset salesman's sample.

Coutil for shapeliness, according to this ad. *Ladies' Home Journal*, September 1895.

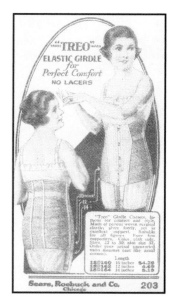

This coutil corset looks anything but comfortable. *Sears & Roebuck*, 1920. Courtesy Sears, Roebuck & Co.

Crash, Linen Toweling and Art Needlework

Thought to be of Russian origin from the word *krashenina* meaning colored linen. Original yarns were tow and /or grey flax (or flax), and jute. More modern crash uses flax and cotton or all cotton, sometimes boiled yarns and other fibers. A plain weave, today's crash is usually of loose, roughly spun yarns. Also tightly twisted but not as absorbent. Yarns of linen, cotton, or union (cotton warp, linen filling), 15" to 20" widths usually in white, half-bleached, natural, or dyed. Also see osnaburg, page 67, and linen, page 56.

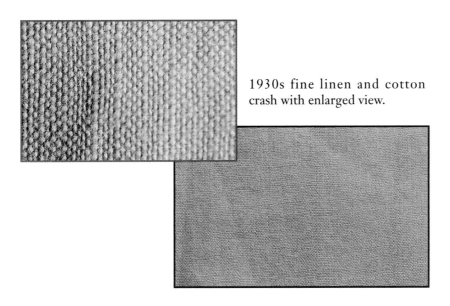

1930s fine linen and cotton crash with enlarged view.

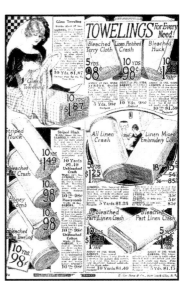

Crash toweling assortment. *Bellas Hess & Co.* 1922 – 1923.

Linene, brand name of a linen-textured crash popular in the 1930s. *Sears & Roebuck*, 1933. Courtesy Sears, Roebuck & Co.

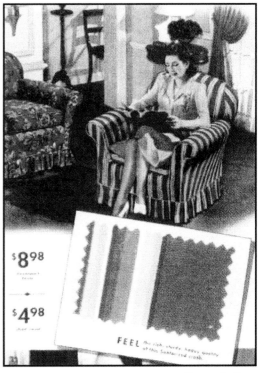

Crash is a durable slipcover fabric. *Sears & Roebuck*, 1942. Courtesy Sears, Roebuck & Co.

Cretonne

Introduced in France in 1650 by Paul Creton of Vitmoutiers, Normandy, a region famous for its linen weavers. At first it was a strong, white fabric with hempen warp and linen filling in plain and twill weaves used for cloaks, garments, and utility. Cretonne is one of many converted forms of osnaburg but it is the chief use of osnaburg today. Cloth ranges from smooth to coarse texture with a fiber range of cotton, linen, rayon, or blends. Glazed, it becomes glazed chintz; textured, barkcloth or pebble cloth; and on occasion will be the base print for upholstery sateen. Primary use is for most home décor fabrics. Fabric is mostly identified with its large floral prints for draperies, slipcovers, and table linen. Also see osnaburg, page 67, and chintz, page 20.

Smooth-surface floral cretonne from a daybed slipcover, late 1930s – early 1940s. Nira Leitzke collection.

For palace or cottage, cretonne created warmth according to Montgomery Ward's 1939 – 1940 catalog.

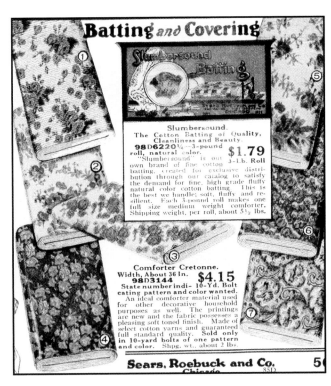

Expendable cretonne — comforter fabric for warmth. *Sears & Roebuck*, 1920. Courtesy Sears, Roebuck & Co. Decorative trim for dresses. *Charles Williams Stores*, 1927. Outdoor chic for the head. *Sears & Roebuck*, 1928. Courtesy Sears, Roebuck & Co. Protection with dust covers. *National Bellas Hess*, 1952.

Dimity

Persian *dimyat, damietta*; also European spellings *dimoty, demyt, dimite, dimmety, dimmity, dimetty, demity, dimitty*; from the Italian *amita, dimitaque,* and *trimita,* meaning fabrics woven with one, two, or three threads respectively. Plain weave, characterized by raised vertical or crossed threads called barres (ribs, cords); soft to crisp finish, usually of fine nainsook, lawn, voile or muslin. Persian cloth was a stout dimity cotton woven with raised stripes or fancy figures and used for beds and garments. Dimity was introduced into Spain by the Moors during their occupation of Iberia around 800 CE. During the fifteenth – sixteenth centuries it was a coarse cotton flannel, and by seventeenth century was a type of course linzie-wolzie (sic). Drapery dimity is heavier, woven in stripes of self-color, usually tan or gray and used for slipcovers and spreads since WWI. Sometimes jaconet is described as a name for a type of crossbarre dimity. Through the 1950s dimity was still advertised as corded dimity when ribs were more pronounced. Dimity was also called corded lawn when made of that fabric with extra raised ribbing.

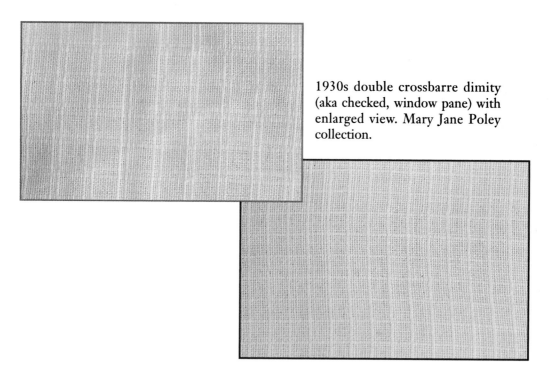

1930s double crossbarre dimity (aka checked, window pane) with enlarged view. Mary Jane Poley collection.

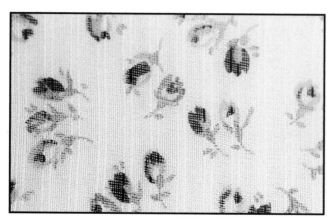

The most beloved and familiar double, vertical barre dimity from the 1940s in the traditional small floral pattern.

Double crossbarre dimity to please a bride. *Bellas Hess & Co.*, 1909. Also see nainsook listing, page 64.

Heavier dimity was ideal for bedspreads. *Montgomery Ward*, 1925. Also see bedspread dimity in seersucker listing, page 83.

Dimity was one of many cool, dainty summer frocks. *Sears & Roebuck*, 1928. Courtesy Sears, Roebuck & Co.

Green printed dimity was suggested for making shorts and brassiere outfit in *Wright's Sewing Booklet #26*, 1932. Courtesy Wm. E. Wright Co.

Dotted Swiss

Developed around 1750 by the Swiss cottage industry in the St. Gall regions, using hand looms with a swivel attachment that tied in dots or designs called hand-tied dots to create a woven raised effect or design of dots or figures on sheer fabric. Yarns on back of cloth are clipped and hand-tied, a process still in practice although power looms have long produced most of this fabric. In early to mid-1800 it was also known as spotted muslin, and a poplar favorite for summery gowns. Plain weave; design most commonly used on lawn, India (or other fine muslin), voile, organdy, nylon, and synthetics for clothing and curtains. See marquisette listing (page 60) for curtains, and "Fabric Identification by Appearance: The Look-alikes" (page 129), for further description and photos of various dotted Swiss types.

Drill, Drilling

Strong twill weave cloths of many kinds and various weights, similar to jean. Name is a shortened form of drilling from the German *drillich*, or three-threaded, which describes drill's weave structure. Made in both linen and cotton, and commonly bleached and finished stiff. Dates at least as far back as seventeenth century. Used for clipper ships' sails, workwear, upholstery/home decor, middy blouses, school and play dresses, rompers, and sportswear.

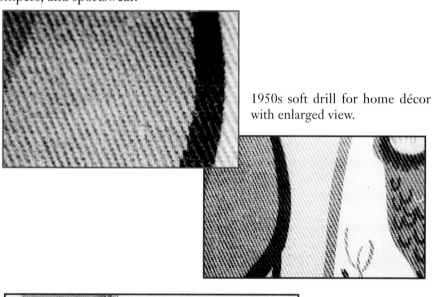

1950s soft drill for home décor with enlarged view.

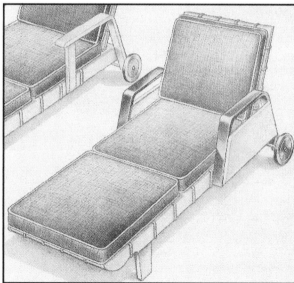

Sturdy drill for home entertainment. *Sears & Roebuck*, 1943. Courtesy Sears, Roebuck & Co.

Drill in wartime casual men's wear. *Sears & Roebuck*, 1943. Courtesy Sears, Roebuck & Co.

Eponge

French for sponge; plain weave, soft, loose fabric similar to ratiné; nubby warp yarns, looped filling yarns. Cotton (shown), silk, wool linen, or linen/20% cotton. Used for dresses and suits suitable for ratiné styles. See ratiné listing, page 79. Currently off-market by this name.

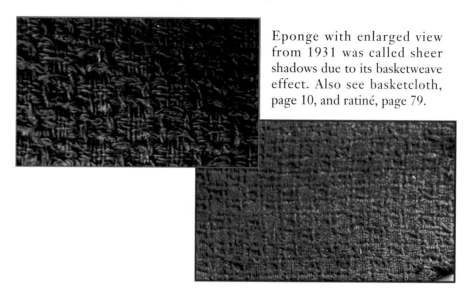

Eponge with enlarged view from 1931 was called sheer shadows due to its basketweave effect. Also see basketcloth, page 10, and ratiné, page 79.

Fancies or Novelties

Fabrics having more than one type of weave, such as plain weave with leno weave for decorative lattice, or fagoting, as found in broadcloths and other cotton shirtings and summery lawns.

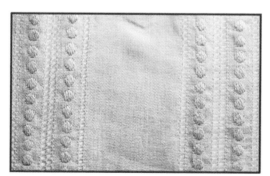

1920s dress-weight fancy fabric uses mock leno and plain weaves to create a chambray effect.

White waisting novelties. *Sears & Roebuck*, 1908. Courtesy Sears, Roebuck & Co.

Feedsack, Feedbag, Grain Sack

Plain weave, also see osnaburg, page 67. Coarse cotton, usually osnaburg bagging but many other cottons used including rayon to attract sewers. Special attractions were theme, novelty, and fancy prints and borders. Bags began to replace barrels during the Civil War and then were gradually replaced by paper and plastic after WWII. Genuine bags distinguished by long machine stitches or large holes where stitching has been removed. Some cotton feedsacks, mostly made for gifts or souvenirs, are still being manufactured.

Feedsacks in wool and cotton were available individually or by the bale. *Sears & Roebuck*, 1897. Courtesy Sears, Roebuck & Co.

1930s – 1940s colorful feedsack prints with enlarged view often were recycled for pillowcases, clothing, curtains, towels and other domestics. Jane Clark Stapel and Betty Wilson collections.

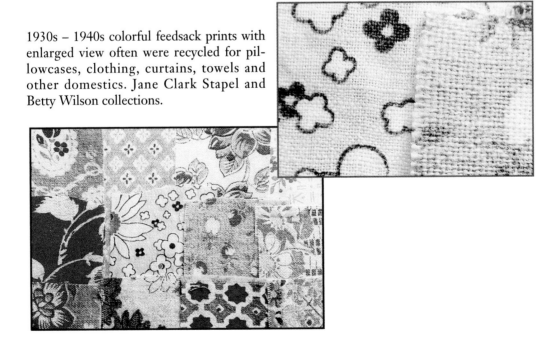

1940s bowtie feedsack quilt with scalloped edges and detail. Pat Cummings collection, photo courtesy James Cummings.

Feedsacks for a variety of uses – three potholders and a pincushion were created from 1930s – 1940s novelty print feedsacks of Mexican and chicken themes. Stuffed doll was made from a 1930s, 100-lb. feedsack which featured printed doll pattern and separate dress and bib. Clothespin bag made from two different 1930s – 1940s sacks. Barbara Garrett collection, photos courtesy Barbara Garrett.

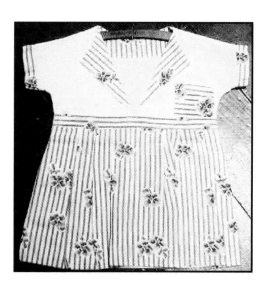

Fine Plain and Print (Standard) Cloths

These are two examples of plain woven grey cloths which are sometimes referred to by those names even in their finished states. They are shown here in a combined presentation because the terms often overlap or can have slightly different meanings at various times.

Print or standard cloth is carded yarn of a good cotton strain with a thread count somewhere between 64x64 up to 140. Fine plain is made from better strain cottons with a higher thread count and is more likely to be combed and mercerized. This cloth deserves a book of its own. Both classifications represesent a vast range of plain-weave cottons which include muslin, percale, lawn, organdy, nainsook, chintz, cretonne, and batiste. Fine plains also refer to those "no-name" fabrics which don't fall into any particular weave pattern which generally give a name to a fabric. Both cloths were (and still are) well known for their serviceability, wash and color fastness, and/or guarantee of quality by manufacturer and need no further identity.

Most of the earlier print or standard cloths were muslin prints (calicoes) of coarser, sturdier yarns which have found their way into the hearts of quilters past and present. Seldom, if at all, were they called muslin but advertised as calicoes, a new wash fabric, staple prints, wash dress goods, wash cottons, colorful prints, serviceable cloth or dress goods, etc., depending on which decade and which catalog was doing the describing. Among the many leading names for finer washfast cottons were American Print Works, Clarion, Columbia, Hope, Merrimack, Simpson, and Washington Prints. Later, brand names respected for their high standard of quality appeared on the market – ABC, Cloth of Gold, Flaxon, Indian Head, Quadriga Cloth, and Soisette, for example, represented the best in everyday cotton and colorful prints.

Fine Plain and Standard Nineteenth Century Dress Goods

Early 1800s fine plains; swatches with turquoise contain linen.

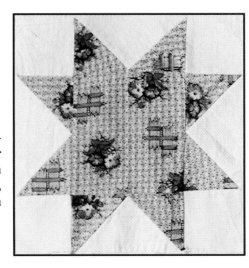

These mid- to late nineteenth century Ohio Star blocks surrounded with a later fabric Cloth of Gold, are begging to be made into a quilt. Judi Fibush collection.

Assortment of standard cloth prints – polka dot cheddar and madder brown, 1865 – 1870; claret, 1880s; and neon blue and brown sprigs with faint wide blue bands, 1890s.

1870s – early 1880s lightly calendered Allen Print Works border print, also called side band. This color combination was popular in the 1870s.

1876 Pennsylvania quilt is an example of centennial print fabrics. Top was restored and repaired, with new borders and backing added, and quilted in 2002. Judy Grow collection, photo courtesy Judy Grow.

1880s colorful, floral dress print by Allen's Print Works. Shirley McElderry collection.

Turkey track quilt, c. 1885, from Franklin County, Pennsylvania, is a mixture of fine plain and standard cloths. Judy Grow collection, photo courtesy Judy Grow.

Charm quilt, c. 1880s, contains more than 1,300 different fabrics, a fabric collector's bonanza. Laurette Carroll collection, photo courtesy Laurette Carroll.

A collection of famous brand names of fine plain and standard cloths, 1880s – early 1900s. Merrimack's striped shirting, Clarion prints, Simpson's linen-finish texture and Silver Greys prints, and American Printing's clarets.

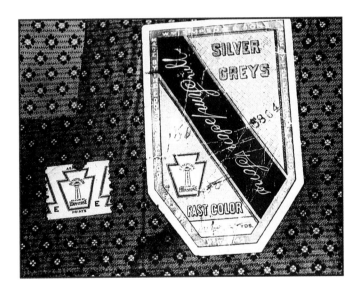

1880s – early 1900s fine plain weaves in popular brown/red themes.

A *Ladies' Home Journal*, February 1896 ad reminds us of the virtue of fine wash goods.

Mint-condition radiating star quilt from upstate New York is a composite of late nineteenth and early twentieth century fabrics; with enlarged view. Sue Reich collection, photo courtesy Sue Reich.

Fine Plain and Standard Twentieth Century Dress Goods

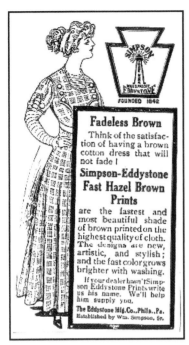

Simpson-Eddystone ad for its fadeless, hazel brown prints. July 1910, *Modern Priscilla*. Shirley McElderry collection.

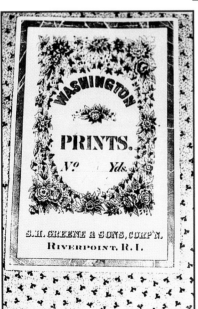

Assorted early 1900s to 1930s brand names of fine plain and standard cloths noted for their quality, luster, special finishes, and easy sewing — American Printing Calcutta prints, Passaic Brocade striping and Washington prints, early 1900s. Soisette colorful prints from 1930s sampler packet. Flaxon, which was noted for its full line of fine staples. *Sears & Roebuck*, 1920. Courtesy Sears, Roebuck & Co.

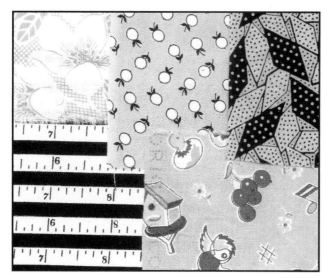

Assortment of fine plain prints — 1930s green and pink florals and figurals, 1930 Soisette Art Deco, 1950s geometrical rulers, and 1940s Soisette whimsical.

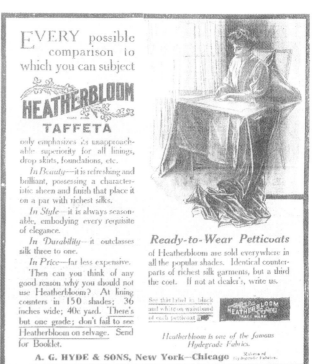

I can't believe it's not silk! Heatherbloom was a silky cotton taffeta fine plain available in 150 shades for making milady's petticoats. *Munsey's Magazine*, February 1908. Ready to wear was also available from Sears & Roebuck's 1920 catalog. Courtesy Sears, Roebuck & Co.

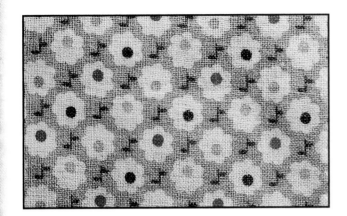

An array of colorful fine-combed and mercerized cottons from 1931.

1940s Quadriga Cloth identified only by its label and "E&W Quadriga." 1953 ad, magazine unknown.

First stop for
new school clothes
...your nearest
Quadriga counter

There you'll find the Fall prints that
give you the go-sign to start sewing!
Take your daughter with you...let her
help choose from Quadriga's dazzling
designs and 53 plain colors. Introduce
her early to this fine cotton fabric that
will be her friend for life . . . so easy to
sew, easy to care for, easy to afford.
Remember "The girl who sews has
better clothes."

SMART MONEY BUYS
E&W
Quadriga Cloth
IT'S NEEDLEIZED

FOR *Color* SECURITY

Your investment in colored shirts, pajamas or shorts
is safe as gilt-edged bonds when the label says "Cranston-Processed."
No matter how or *how often* you suds or sun them, they stay
steadfast to their brightness, look fresh as the day you bought them.
So when you buy, always look for the label saying "Cranston-Processed."
Cranston Print Works Company, Cranston, R. I., Established 1825.

A
CRANSTON-PROCESSED
FABRIC

Be sure! be secure! say "CRANSTON PROCESSED" for
● PERMANENT COLORS ● PERMANENT FIT
● TOP QUALITY FABRIC

Cranston-processed fine plains as
advertised in *Saturday Evening Post*,
June 14, 1947. Courtesy Cranston
Print Works Company™.

Another fine plain from the 1940s, Lancaster Prints
by Springs Cotton Mills. Courtesy White Homestead
Archives/Springs Industries.

Flannelette

Plain weave, soft cotton, lightly napped on one or both sides, usually printed. Kimono flannel changed to flannelette around 1923. For infant's sleepwear, tea gowns, wrappers, and kimonos. Also a dress fabric called fleece, usually printed with light nap on wrong side, to make shirtwaists or children's clothes. See Cocheco fleece swatch, below. Sears featured fleece in its 1908 catalog.

Late 1890s – early 1900s Cocheco weave jacquard fleece waist flannel lightly napped on reverse side. Shirley McElderry collection.

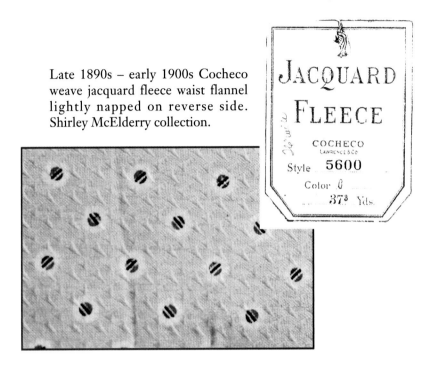

1909 Hamilton's Lerma brand dress or waisting flannel print with lightly napped reverse side. Shirley McElderry collection.

1940s whimsical puppy print, double napped (napped on both sides) for extra warmth.

His 'n' hers flannel nightwear. *Bellas Hess*, 1909.

The perfect cold weather ensemble: flannelette night suit with matching hood and socks, and for an added bonus, a drop seat. *Sears & Roebuck*, 1920. Courtesy Sears, Roebuck & Co.

A cozy flannelette wrapper with corduroy trim. *Charles Williams Stores*, 1927.

Some styles will always remain popular such as the flannel granny gown. *Montgomery Ward*, 1950.

Galatea

Satin and twill weaves, heavy cotton similar to drill. While warm as wool and popular for children's winter wear and play clothes and middies, galatea faded and shrunk, and whites were difficult to keep from yellowing. Off-market by end of WWII.

1920s salesman's galatea sample swatch book of Moneyworth Fabric's Ironclad brand.

Galatea striped dress in a bargain combination offer from Standard Mail Order Co. *Pictorial Review*, May 1914.

Gauze

Plain weave, not to be confused with gauze weave, an outdated name for leno or doup weave. A timeless favorite which dates back to the early looms of India. Gauze is usually an umbrella name for loosely woven sheers. Also a term for thin, light openwork or open mesh for summer dresses or for gossamer (a very thin, strong, soft gauze). Loosely woven lawns and fine muslins are often referred to as gauzies. Also made in silk and linen.

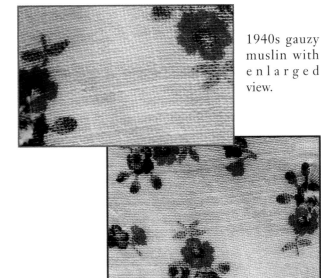

1940s gauzy muslin with enlarged view.

Two c. WWI gauzy lawn prints.

Gingham

Malaysian, *ging-gang* meaning striped. French – *guingan*, Spanish – *guinga*, Potuguese – *guingao*, Italian – *gingano*. First recorded in England in early seventeenth century. Plain weave woven from yarn-dyed fast colors, better grades combed. When woven in two colors, gingham is called checked; three or more colors, plaid. Varies in quality depending on type of yarn; uses range from feedsack to fine tissue cloth. Printed check pattern is known as imitation gingham or print gingham. Varieties are: Apron check – coarse and stiff; Nurses or Red Cross – heavy blue and white stripe; Scotch – fine quality, beautiful colors and plaids; Tissue – thin, lightweight, soft finish, attractive coloring and designs; Standard – dresses, rompers, play clothes, uniforms; and Umbrella – usually solid black, made for umbrella covers. Everett and Toile du Nord were Montgomery Ward brands. Ward's also sold Aberfoyle zephyrs in its 1897 catalog. Asmoskeag and Anderson brands sold in Sears 1902 catalog. Kaliburnie was another prominent brand. Springs Mills and Dan River also produced fine ginghams in their formative years.

1920s fancy gingham similar to those in Montgomery Ward's 1926 catalog.

Classic 1931 super-fine, silky-finish gingham plaid with enlarged view.

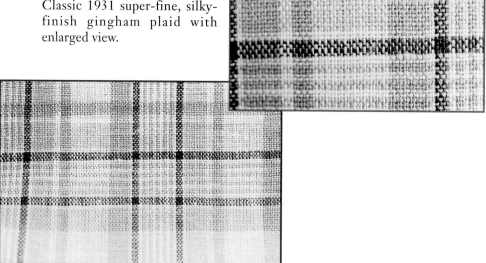

1950s quality floral flocking on semi-sheer gingham. Dolores Lambert collection.

Gingham throughout time — Flowing in *Ladies' Home Journal*, March 1896. Sturdy for family work and play, with stylish flair. *Sears & Roebuck*, 1920 and 1933. Courtesy Sears, Roebuck & Co.

Granite Cloth

Fancy weave; also called woven crepe, worsted or cotton crepe; hard-finish pebbly texture resembling granite; fancy or irregular weave, hard wearing. Similar to and often interchangeable with momie cloth. Popular from WWI on and a fashion favorite in the 1930s. Granite cloth appears from time to time, but by other names, according to fashion dictates. Also see wool section, page 110. Currently off-market by this name.

1930s – early 1940s granite cloths with their helter skelter weaves. Shown with a fancy granite-type crepe weave fashionably called Exposition when introduced in 1951. Courtesy White Homestead Archives/Springs Industries. Also see granite and crepe ad in wool section, page 110, and ratiné, page 79.

Cotton and wool granite cloth dress. *Sears & Roebuck*, 1920. Courtesy Sears, Roebuck & Co.

Grenadine

Leno weave, silk or cotton gauze, sometimes figured; popular in early 1800s – 1860s. Mainly used for dresses and shawls. Hernani was an offshoot, originally a silk and wool grenadine which became a thin, light silk between gauze and grenadine. Black silk grenadine sold in Sears 1897 catalog. Grenadine is a finer mesh than its cousin, marquisette. Currently off-market by this name, it exists today as a sheer curtain fabric. This is where a linen tester comes in handy. See "Fabric Identification by Appearance: The Look-alikes," page 128.

This modern grenadine with enlarged view is called a fancy organza by its manufacturer but it is actually an allover leno weave which creates the shadow-stripe effect.

Silk and cotton grenadine was sold through Aberfoyle Mfg. Co. *Ladies' Home Journal,* January 1896.

The Goods that Wash the Best and Wear the Longest

Grenadine Suissé
the three essentials of a smart gown
Lustrous Fabric
Light Weight
Brilliant Colors

Silk and cotton, but you only see the silk. The cotton is there for firmness.

Latest Novelty of the
ABERFOYLE
MFG. CO.

Cool and delicate Edwardian grenadine dress for summer wear. It graces the cover of this book. Dawna Ellenberger collection.

Grenadine dotted Swiss curtains create a cozy setting. *Sears & Roebuck*, 1943. Courtesy Sears, Roebuck & Co.

Himalaya Cloth or Cotton Shantung

Plain weave, highly mercerized; also referred to as a type of poplin. Imitates pongee, a smooth or rough texture which is called shantung. Known by this name in the 1920s – 1930s but as cotton shantung thereafter.

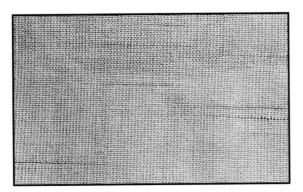

Fine, supple Himalaya cloth from 1931 which looks and feels like its silk counterpart; notice shantung-type crossgrain random slubbing.

Cotton shantung broadcloth varieties. *Montgomery Ward,* 1939.

Indian Head

Plain weave, specially woven superior muslin with permanent finish linen texture, also a line of fine percales and broadcloths; colorfast, preshrunk. Dates back to 1834 when first introduced by Jackson Mills as a sheeting. In 1916 mills were acquired by Nashua Mfg. Co. which sold Indian Head to Textron in 1945. During 1953 Textron sold its Indian Head Division and the new company became Indian Head Mills. See "Fabric Identification by Width, Brand Names, Finishes, and Mills," pages 137 & 147. Indian Head fabric discontinued in 1961.

Indian Head sample packets from 1934 and 1939 with enlarged view are combed and mercerized with a wonderful sheen. Finesse compares to broadcloth, and might have been the brand name for Nashua's line when it introduced broadcloth in 1934.

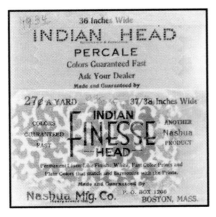

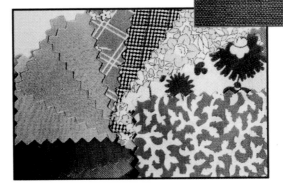

Logo-speak — late 1940s – 1952 floral with
Indian Head Cloth imprinted in selvage
denotes fabric was made prior to Textron's
sale in 1953 to the newly formed Indian
Head Mills. Mid-1950s nursery print with
Indian Head Mills printed in selvage
denotes new ownership.

Smock a Frock

A child's dress made of Indian Head,
prettily smocked, is one of the most pleasing
styles you could choose. Indian Head has
a firm, round thread that makes it very easy
to embroider, smock or use for the drawn
work which is to be so fashionable this year.

INDIAN HEAD

Reg. U. S. Pat. Off.

27, 33, 36, 40 and 44 inches wide
12½ to 25c a yard

This material is not only unusually attractive but is
thoroughly practical for dresses for yourself and the
children. It costs much less than linen, keeps fresh
and clean a long time and does not wrinkle. Indian
Head always keeps the friends it makes, and they use
it year after year with increasing satisfaction. Ask
your dealer to show it to you and look
for the words "Indian Head" on the
selvage.

A Useful Sample
FREE

Write for doll's dress of Indian
Head, cut ready to sew with directions. State whether for 14, 16 or
18 inch doll.

Amory, Browne & Co.

Dept. 23   48 Franklin St., Boston, Mass.

Indian Head magazine
ads 1915 and c. 1934.
Pat L. Nickols collec-
tion.

Blotters were household staples essential to drying writing made by fountain pens until the ballpoint took over in the 1960s. These absorbent-backed cards were a heaven-made medium for advertising. Indian Head was no exception to promoting its fabrics in this 1920 blotter. Pat Cummings collection, photo courtesy James Cummings.

1953 Indian Head embroidered luncheon display set with enlarged view to promote kits sold at department and fabric stores. Mary Connell collection.

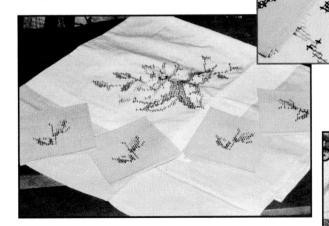

A bit of nostalgia — this might have been one of the final appearances of Indian Head, as fabric was discontinued in 1961. *Montgomery Ward*, 1961.

Interlinings, Stiffeners and Shapers

Paper, cloth, and hair fabrics which were needed to help garments retain their shape. Essential for 1890s – Edwardian 1900s sleeves, skirts and capes. See plush listing (page 76) for photo of interlining. These were some of the major brands available from late 1880s – early 1900s: Fibre Chamois, uncrushable, shape retentive, elastic pliancy in 3 weights; #10 light for collars; #20 medium for skirts and jackets; #30 for heavy items. Used on mutton sleeves for bouffant effect and for retaining godet flares. Name stamped in selvage, 64" wide. Hair Cloth, hair filling, warp cotton, elastic and resilient, no stretch, 64" wide. Sponge Crepon, a stiffening similar to Fiber Chamois, 64" wide. Cheveret interlining, resilient, non-tearing.

Stiffeners such as Fibre Chamois and Cheveret were integral shaping components to keep mutton-leg sleeves poofy and skirts and capes flaring. *Ladies' Home Journal*, May 1895 and January 1896. Also see plush listing, page 76.

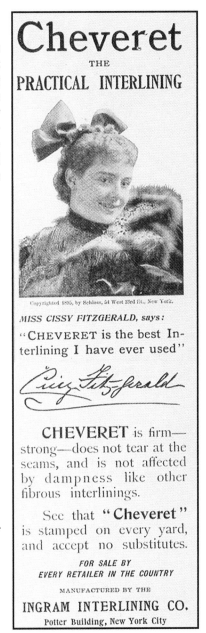

Fine-quality crinoline pleated edging for adding oomph to underskirt flouncings in the Edwardian – WWI era.

Jaconet
See lawn listing below.

Kimono Cloth
Plain weave; permanently grooved ridges give crepe paper appearance. Popular around WWI into 1940s. Used for kimonos and loungewear. Currently making a comeback for outer wear.

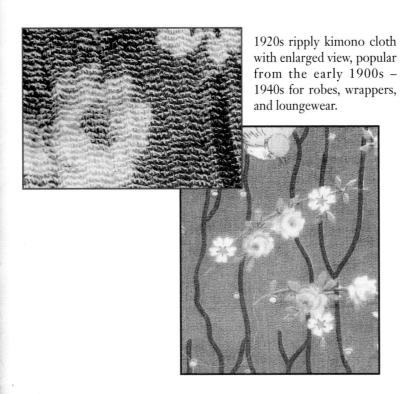

1920s ripply kimono cloth with enlarged view, popular from the early 1900s – 1940s for robes, wrappers, and loungewear.

Cotton crepe in an attractive morning house wrapper. 1920 Sears catalog. Courtesy Sears, Roebuck & Co.

Lawn, Fr. Linon
The word lawn was formerly derived from the French name for the fabric linon, from lin, flax, linen, but Skeat (Etym. Diet., 1898, Addenda) and A. Thomas (Romania, XXIX. 582, 1900) have shown that the real source of the word is to be found in the name of the French town Laon. Skeat quotes from Palsgrave, Les claircissement de la langue Franco~se (1530), showing that the early name of the fabric was Laune lynen. An early form of the word was laund, probably due to an adaptation to laund, lawn, glade or clearing in a forest, now used for a closely-mown expanse of grass in a garden, park, etc. Plain weave; sheer to semi-sheer of fine yarns often combed, mercerized, and given a crisp finish known as lawn finish. Part of the batiste, mull nainsook family; used for summer dresses, handkerchiefs, and linings. The following are various types of lawn that were available during 1880s – 1959: Bishop lawn – heavier lawn used for certain portions of the dress of bishops and other ecclesiastical garments, hence the name. 1880s – Edwardian era. Also see mull, page 61. Cobweb lawn – as the name indicates it is a fine gauzy variety. 1880s – Edwardian era. Cypress lawn – name formerly applied to black lawn for mourning purposes, and at one time was identical to black cotton crepe; so called due to cypress branches having anciently been used at funerals as emblems of grief. 1880s – Edwadian era; India linon – light, thin cotton, highly polished, soft or stiff finish; fine, and crisp, a substitute for organdy (later called lawn organdy). Coarse grade called lining lawn. For dresses, slips, waists, aprons, curtains, linings; Jaconet, Jaconet lawn – French, *jaconnet, jaconette, jaconnot*, from the Hindi *jagannath*, an East Indian cloth as it is more a type of lawn. Depending upon the time in history one runs across this fabric, it will have varying descriptions ranging from a fine, sheer cotton highly polished on right side or with a soft finish resembling nainsook; thinner than nainsook, thinner than lawn, thinner than cambric, same as lawn, between lawn and

cambric, same as cambric, heavier than cambric to an even heavier cloth given a hard finish for bookbinding. Possibly this latter cloth is the same as modern book cambric. In Edwardian times, it was often called jaconet lawn; Lawn organdy – permanent starchless finishes to lawn, batiste, and fine muslin to give body and to simulate organdy but without the stiffness. A popular term in late 1940s – 1950s; Persian lawn – sheer, white polished cotton; thinner and finer than India lawn, stiffer and firmer than batiste, not as sheer as organdy. For waists, lingerie, blouses, dresses, neckwear, infant's dresses. 1880s – Edwardian era; Victoria lawn – white cotton lawn, made in many qualities, named in honor of England's Queen Victoria. 1880s – Edwardian era; Thread lawn – pure linen lawn, and is sometimes called Irish lawn. The term originated in the eighteenth century to designate an all-linen from a mixed lawn, just as thread lace is used to describe an all-linen lace as distinguished from one made of cotton. 1880s – Edwardian era. See "Fabric Identification by Appearance: The Look-alikes," page 128 for information on lawn organdy and Swiss muslin.

Early 1900s Swiss muslin made of lawn rather than fine India muslin; red warp and white filling create a chambray look.

Lawn assortment — early 1900s Art Nouveau, c. WWI Schreinerized (highly calendered) warp print, 1920s paisley, 1930s soft colors and 1940s fine corded.

Late 1880s – early 1900 cotton net over-dress is lavishly decorated with satin stitch embroidered lawn front panel. Longer back skirt indicates dress was worn with a padded bustle. Handmade by an English seamstress for a Pennsylvania family. Old Mill Village Museum collection. Photo courtesy Linda Learn.

1890s lawn blouse on gown trimmed with yards of lace insertion and embroidery. Dawna Ellenberger collection. Photo courtesy Linda Learn.

1890s tea garden attire – yellow and dark grey printed lawn trimmed with black lace. Old Mill Village Museum collection. Photo courtesy Linda Learn.

Jaconet lawn was the trendy fabric in the 1890s. *Ladies' Home Journal*, June 1895.

Swiss muslin was often a lawn. *Ladies' Home Journal*, April 1895. See "Fabric Identification by Appearance: The Look-alikes," page 128.

1930s sheer lawn formal is reminiscent of those worn at college proms in MGM movies. Old Mill Village Museum collection. Photo courtesy Linda Learn.

APPROVAL SAMPLE

SPRINGS BLEACHERY
GRACE, S. C.
TO

SPRINGS MILLS, INC.
200 CHURCH STREET
NEW YORK 13, N. Y.

QUALITY 39" 74x86 4.75
                          S/351
SHADE White
FINISH M̈ercerized
            Sanforized
WIDTH 34/35
LOT NO. 600
DATE 2-9-49
Comb̶̶̶̶̶̶̶̶̶̶̶̶̶iel Lawn
Regular Twist

Converted lawn sample for final approval before marketing, 1949. Courtesy White Homestead Archives/Springs Industries.

Linen

From Old English. Recorded as linen since 700 CE and from Germanic word roots *linom*. Plain weave fabric; thread or yarn made from flax. One of the oldest textile fibers known, dating back to ancient Egypt. Lustrous, heavy, fine, smooth. Needs little sizing; finest quality from Belgium. Long fibers called line, short are tow. Tow is used in low-grade fabrics and twine. Bis and byse were names for sixteenth and seventeenth century silky linen as was Holland linen, a multi-purpose cloth in many weights for clothing and bedding. There were many cotton imitations of linen such as linno cloth, linene, and butcher linen, a rayon. Also see crash, page 23.

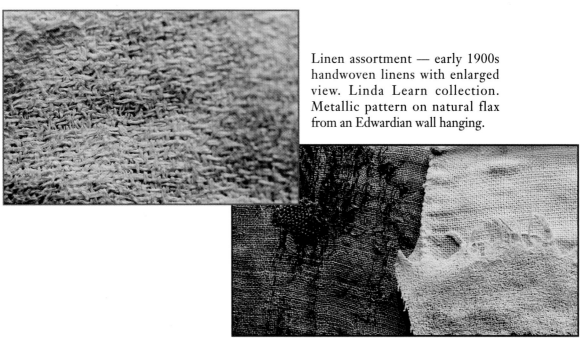

Linen assortment — early 1900s handwoven linens with enlarged view. Linda Learn collection. Metallic pattern on natural flax from an Edwardian wall hanging.

1930s dress linen, suiting-weight linen, and linen/cotton blends.

Looking as modern as today, a slimming floral linen dress of block-printed design c. 1790-1810. Courtesy American Textile History Museum.

Grass cloth, woven of ramie fibers, was often called grass linen and substituted for linen because of its similar physical properties. *Ladies' Home Journal*, July 1896.

Finely detailed linen blouses. *Bellas Hess & Co.*, 1909.

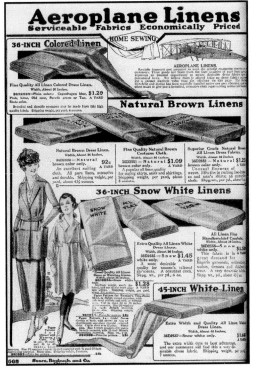

Linen for every use from aeroplanes to clothes. *Sears & Roebuck*, 1920. Courtesy Sears, Roebuck & Co.

Linsey-Woolsey (Linsey)

Coarse, loosely woven from linen warp and wool filling; dates to middle ages. First made in Linsey, England, in linen-wool blend. There are many versions of the spelling of the name, including Lindsey Woolzey and Linzey Woolzey. See cottsey-woolsey, page 22.

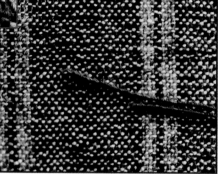

Rough and tweedy linsey-woolsey with enlarged view is currently made by specialty artisans in the same centuries-old traditional manner.

Longcloth, Plain Weave

Fine, soft-twist yarn, lightweight, unfinished muslin; bleached, little or no sizing or starch. So named as it was one of the first fabrics woven in long pieces. Related to batiste/lawn family, similar to fine muslin. For undergarments, linings, and infant's wear; also sheeting and quilt backings. Currently off-market by this name.

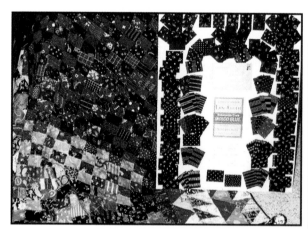

Longcloth of a different color — sample pack of indigo prints and label closeup from Arnold Print Works Co., 1887, printed on longcloth spelled as two words. Swatches are mounted for use as a teaching aid for textile study. Quilt contains many of the samples. (See "Stifel Cloth and Other Indigoes," page 84.) Xenia Cord collection. Photos courtesy Xenia Cord.

Early 1900s – WWI fine chamois (soft) finish longcloth for under-muslins bear the Barnsley and Quaker Lady labels. Shirley McElderry collection.

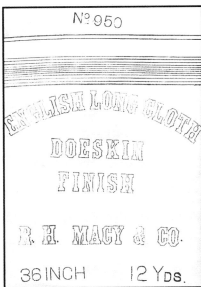

1930s – 1940s longcloth with doeskin (soft) finish. This fabric is coarser grade and finish washes out, leaving fabric limp and unattractive.

Superior grade longcloth for clothing. *Sears & Roebuck*, 1920. Courtesy Sears, Roebuck & Co.

Fine-grade longcloth was ideal for chemises. *Bellas Hess & Co.*, 1922 – 1923.

Marquisette

A mesh of leno construction often confused with plain weaves such as scrim and voile. Its larger mesh distinguishes it from grenadine. Cotton was fiber of choice followed by rayon, wool, and silk. Mostly in nylon and other synthetics today and primarily used for curtains. During the 1930s – 1950s was popular as an overskirt for dressy occasions. See "Fabric Identitification by Appearance: The Look-alikes," page 128, for photo and further description.

Marquisette is probably best known as a favorite curtain fabric. *National Bellas Hess*, 1946 – 1947. See "Fabric Identification by Appearance: The Look-alikes," page 128.

Monk's Cloth

Basket weave, hopsacking with origins to middle ages; 2x2 basketweave (two warps over two fillings), similar to friar's cloth 4x4 and druid cloth 6x8. Also called cloister cloth, mission cloth, abbot cloth. Rough, heavy yarns can also be flax, jute, or hemp. For couch covers, hangings, and draperies.

The various types of basketweave found in monk's cloth — 8-ply would be comparable to druid cloth. *Sears & Roebuck*, 1943. Courtesy Sears, Roebuck & Co.

Fancy plaid monk's cloth curtains make attractive window dressing. *Sears & Roebuck*, 1943. Courtesy Sears, Roebuck & Co.

Mull

From Hindu *mullmul* or Persian *malmal* or *malmul* which means muslin. A soft, plain Bengalese muslin. During the seventeenth century it was exported from India to England as an embroidered cloth, sometimes in gold or silver, for petticoats. A plain weave, more opaque than lawn and sheerer than nainsook, it was originally of extremely fine yarns and zephyr quality and later made in many varieties and grades in bleached and pastels. Formerly used in several grades for summer dresses and children's wear. Still popular in Great Britain. China mull — a blend of cotton and silk. India and French mull — cotton for under-muslins and lingerie, nightwear, pillowcases, flouncing, infant's and children's wear, and dresses or gowns when in fashion and suitable. Rayon mull — also in blends for dresses. Silk mull — for millinery and neck-wear. Seco® was a brand name during the 1920s – 1930s. Swiss or starched mull — coarser yarns resembling lawn, lining for underlinings, and heavily sized for millinery interlinings and in bookbinding. Bishop's lawn — a heavier cotton used for ecclesiastical vestments. Also see lawn, page 52.

1930s eyelet border mull; 30" wide yardage, perfect for pillowcases, children's clothes, and fine undergarments.

Mull was a desired fabric for undermuslims. *Ladies' Home Journal*, July 1895.

Muslin Dress and Bed Sheeting

Named for place of origin, Mosul, Kurdistan, in present day Iraq. Firm weave cotton heavier and stronger than longcloth. In England, fabric refers to sheers or India muslin for summer wear. Dress muslin — see photos in fine plain and calico listings, pages 14 & 37. Good to top-grade quality for clothing in plains and prints, and the backbone of many type cottons such as calico dress prints. Merrimack, Hamilton, and Simpson brand wash dress prints sold in Sears 1902 catalog. Used for skirts, dresses, middy blouses, and underwear. Seerhand muslin — quality muslin in a weight between nainsook and mull and which fits description of longcloth. Bed sheeting — heavy white or unbleached muslin, percale (often referred to as fine-grade muslin), broadcloth, or linen. Twill weave used by hospitals for greater strength. Better grades closely woven and firm; poor grades heavily sized. Used for pillowcases, uniforms, and aprons. Linen sheeting stays cleaner, more durable but unsuitable as it holds moisture. Used mostly now for skirts, uniforms, tablecloths, and napkins. The average household made its own sheets; ready-made was too expensive. Some popular sheet brands — Aurora, Dan River, Dwight Anchor, Dwight Star, Fruit of the Loom, Lockwood, Pepperell, Pequot, Pocahontas, Springmaid, and Utica.

Some early 1890s muslin sheeting brands – Belle Isle and Hopewell Bleachery. Shirley McElderry collection. E & W stampings from an end bolt and Creston and Merit salesman's sample packs. Xenia Cord collection. Photos courtesy Xenia Cord.

Pequot sheets stayed white and whole according to its manufacturer. *Pictorial Review*, May 1914.

Springmaid sheets, including luxury muslin, caused a sensation in the late 1940s – 1950s due to a smash advertising campaign with clever ads and promos such as playing cards. The "Be Protected" ad promotes a special cotton fabric developed by Springs Cotton Mills during WWII. Called Kerba, combed broadcloth was water repellant and wind resistant, used at first for ski pants and Arctic uniforms and later for bedding. Courtesy White Homestead Archives/Springs Industries.

Nainsook, Nyansook, Nansook

From the Hindi *nainsukh* meaning "eye delight or pleasure to the eye." Developed in seventeenth century India, cloth is often referred to as opaque or coarse batiste resembling but heavier than jaconet. A plain weave woven in whites or soft pastels in plain, plaids, stripes, and corded checks, also called checked nainsook, barred muslin, or pajama dimity; the latter very popular for children's and men's nightwear in the 1920s. Related to batiste, jaconet, lawn, and mull. English nainsook has a soft finish; French nainsook is calendered or lightly starched and resembles cambric.

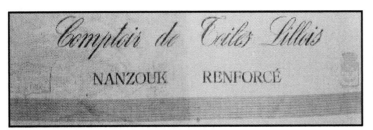

French nainsook, c. WWI, with a calendered finish resembles cambric more than the traditional semi-sheer English nainsook. Lillian Menzies collection.

Nainsook's softness made it a favorite for baby garments and adult sleepwear. *Bellas Hess*, 1922 and *Chicago Mail Order Co.*, 1934.

Organdy, Organdie, Organdee

Plain weave, wiry, lightweight and sheerest cotton made of lawn, muslin, voile, and synthetics; transparent called Swiss organdy. Characterized by its stiff finish; top grades are washable and retain permanent stiffness. Finest have Swiss Herberlein finish which is often mistaken for starchless lawns. See "Fabric Identification by Appearance: The Look-alikes," page 128.

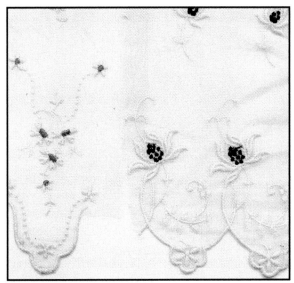

Early 1900s semi-transparent organdy with Art Nouveau embroidered edgings.

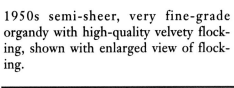

1930s semi-transparent organdy with alternating rows of embroidered dots and eyelets.

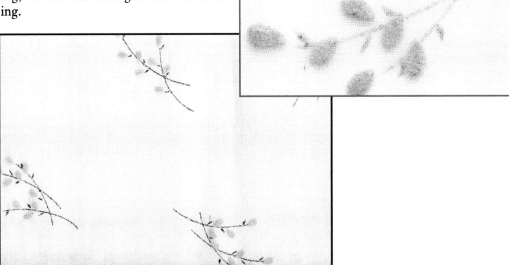

1950s semi-sheer, very fine-grade organdy with high-quality velvety flocking, shown with enlarged view of flocking.

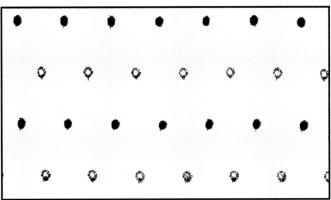

Organdy's permanent crispness made it an ideal fabric for accessories like these 1930s petal bunches for hair or dress decoration, and collar and cuff sets from *Sears & Roebuck*, 1943. Courtesy Sears, Roebuck & Co.

Organdy flock dot frock. *Chicago Mail Order Co.*, 1934.

Osnaburg

Woven originally of coarse linen when introduced around fifteenth century in Osnabruck, Germany from which fabric is named. Current name a corruption of English spelling. Formerly spelled Osenbrege, Ossenbrydge, Ostenbriges, Ozenbridg(e), Osburow, Osenbrigs, Oz-Osnabrigs-brug, Ozenbrigs, Ossenburgs, and Osnaburgh. Mother of barkcloth, chintz, crash, cretonne, and feedsacks, all of which can be seen in this section. Plain weave, coarse yarn, medium to heavy-weight cloth woven of part-waste, low-grade cotton or short-staple, low-grade cotton. Usually thought of as a utility and coarse feedbag fabric, few people realize how many "children" osnaburg has created. In grey state it is used for mattress covers, feedbags, and, before synthetics it was used for imitation leathers and tire linings. Converted it becomes pocketing, cretonne, crash, and hopsacking.

Percale

Possibly from Persian pargalah, a rag. Modern percale originated in France as a linen and was sometimes called French cambric. Spelled perkale elsewhere in the seventeenth and eighteenth centuries. Plain weave, higher thread count than muslin, often combed and mercerized and given a cambric finish. Introduced in America in about 1865 to provide a finer plain weave than muslin; often known as American percale. Some 1880s – early 1900s fine-quality percale surprisingly feels and looks like a cross between lawn and tissue gingham but is slightly crisper. It was described in the 1890s as lacking gloss, its dull surface not being subjected to any pressure during the finishing process. Just the opposite of what would distinguish this fabric later on with its lustrous surface. Sears sold the famous Mulhouse brand in its 1902 catalog; cambric finish in the 1933 catalog, and collectively called its finest percale cambrics. See thread count chart in "Buying, Pricing, and Thread count," page 115.

1850s excellent quality percale used for dress lining. See dress in mousseline delaine wool section, page 108.

Famous turn-of-the-century percale brand names – Liberty Bell prints, Hamilton waistings.

Famous percale brand names – Algonquin's Columbia gauzy prints, Trojan semi sheer prints and Dolly Madison striping and polka dots. From the early 1900s. Shirley McElderry collection.

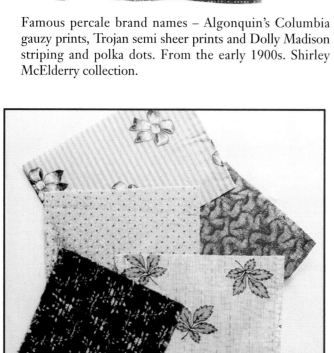

1880s percales apt to be called fine washable goods in catalogs and stores.

80 sq. (160 thread count) percales from a 1934 scrap-bag quilt kit.

Fancy pleated men's percale shirts. *Bellas Hess*, 1909.

The indispensable percale housedress. *Sears & Roebuck*, 1920. Courtesy Sears, Roebuck & Co. Apron, *Farm & Home*, October 1922. Polly Prim was a respected brand name.

Cool and colorful percale lounging pajamas. *Chicago Mail Order Co.*, 1934.

Piqué and Bedford Cord (Cloth)

Corded, fancy weaves. Piqué – true piqué had cords in the filling direction and was thus described in glossaries to about the mid-1920s. This crossgrain ribbing made it easy to distinguish fabric from Bedford cord with its wider and smoother lengthwise ribs. Due to the slimming features of warp ribbing and economy in weaving, piqué ribbing was converted to lengthwise cords in the 1920s. Piqué is usually mercerized, ribs vary in width, and wider ribs are often mistaken for Bedford cord.

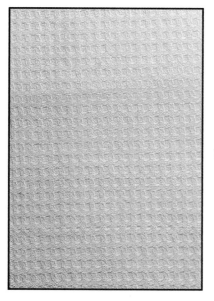

1930s combed and mercerized fancy birdseye piqué.

1940s honeycomb or diamond piqué with enlarged view.

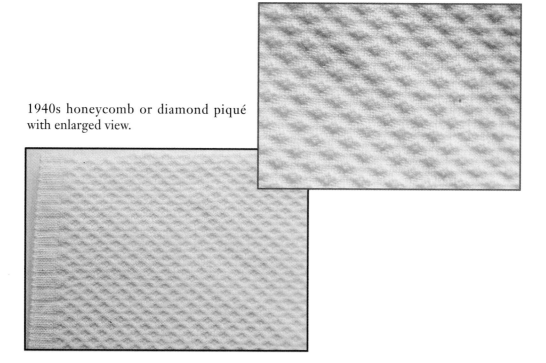

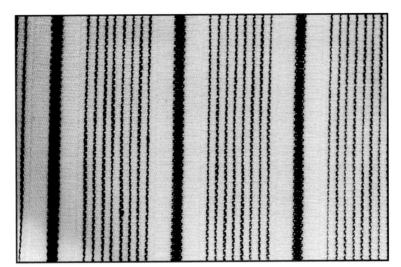

1940s fancy wale piqué.

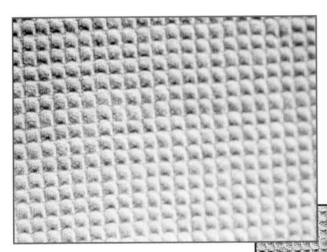

1950s combed waffle piqué with enlarged view.

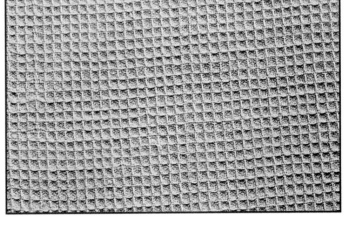

Late 1950s fancy or cloqué piqués. White is cotton, pink is Dacron which was relatively new to the market at that time.

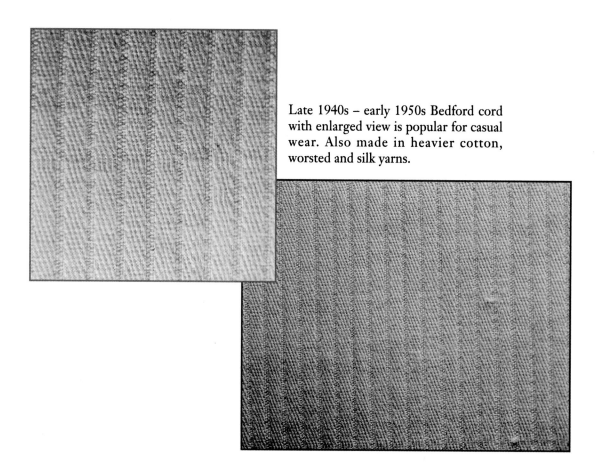

Late 1940s – early 1950s Bedford cord with enlarged view is popular for casual wear. Also made in heavier cotton, worsted and silk yarns.

Green piqué costume with heavy wales and fine crosslines to form a plaid effect. *Ladies' Home Journal*, May 1896.

Child's Bedford cloth coat ensemble shown with a cotton cashmere coat. *Sears & Roebuck*, 1920. Courtesy Sears, Roebuck & Co.

Smart piqué suit. *Chicago Mail Order Co.*, 1934.

Birdseye and other textured piqués reigned throughout the 1950s. *Montgomery Ward*, 1957.

Plissé

Plain weave; puckered or blistered striping or crinkle effect chemically applied in finishing process; cloth is usually various grades of muslin. Often mistaken for seersucker. Kimono crepe is creped in grooves and resembles crepe paper. A favorite brand, Serpentine Crepe, was listed in a late 1880s Montgomery Ward catalog. A fashion fabric of 1902 was called tucked plissé. It resembled plissé or seersucker striping but was not related, the plissé being used in its French context for plaited or pleated. Another brand was Plissé Crepe, a lightweight, thin, pinstripe for an allover blistery effect. See "Fabric Identification by Appearance: The Look-alikes," page 128.

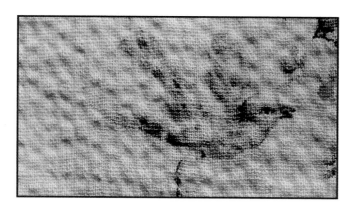

1920s traditional puckered striping plissé of soft, semi-gauzy muslin with the favorite bluebird motif of that era.

1930s plissé of allover crinkle crepe in a whimsical mother goose print with enlarged view.

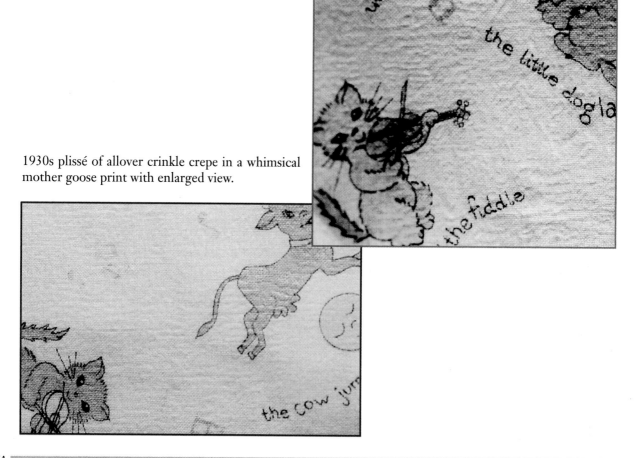

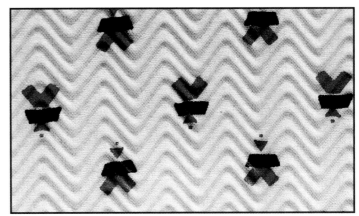

1940s – 1950s polished embossed plissé in sailor design.

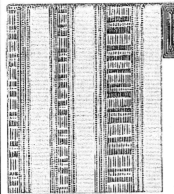

An early plissé which was pleated rather than blistered as in modern plissé. The name was used in true sense of the French word *plissé* for pleated. *Sears & Roebuck*, 1902. Courtesy Sears, Roebuck & Co.

Easy-care plissé bedroom ensemble. *Montgomery Ward*, 1957.

Plush, Pile

Pile is ⅛" or longer than plush; from the French *peluche* meaning shaggy. An old fabric dating back to at least sixteenth century when it had a shorter pile than velvet and was softer. Also called dogskin in the 1870s – 1880s.

1890s cotton plush from a cape with felted paper interlining and wide selvage. Interlining is similar to description of Fibre Chamois and Cheveret in interlining listing and in brand names, "Fabric Identification by Width, Brand Names, Finishes, & Mills."

Modern version of plush cape was the Jacquette. *Chicago Mail Order Co.*, 1934.

Plush capes in cotton and silk with faux fur trim were a staple part of 1890s wardrobes. *Ladies' Home Journal*, September 1896.

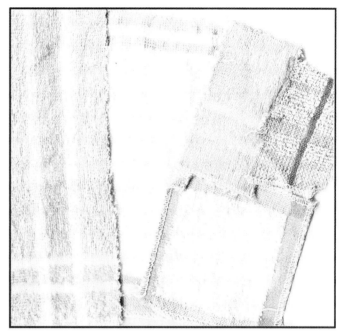

Terrycloth, a relative of plush, is esteemed for its warmth and absorbancy for home use and wear, and to delight little girls playing house. Commercial and handmade towels and washcloths made for a 1920s – early 1930s doll's wash stand.

1930s powder puff plush, essential for compacts and toilettes and to be encased in delicately crocheted covers for traveling and gift-giving.

Poplin

Frank Bennett's *A Cotton Fabrics Glossary* noted in its 1914 edition that mercerized poplin represented a line of fabric noted for its beauty, value and the wide variety of uses. He predicted that the future of this fabric would make it the most important staple fancy cloth on the market. Poplin is a plain weave, fine, filling-ribbed cotton, usually mercerized. Same as broadcloth but heavier weight and with more pronounced slubbing in filling yarns. In UK, broadcloth is called poplin. See himalaya cloth, page 48.

Poplin fashion print, from 1931, with enlarged view, often used for pajamas and loungewear.

Poplin shows its versatility in loungewear (*Sears & Roebuck*, 1943. Courtesy Sears, Roebuck & Co.) and in sportswear (*Montgomery Ward*, 1952 and 1957.)

Ratiné

Fancy or crepe weave; rough, loosely woven from specially prepared yarns which give either a nubby or spongy appearance, sometimes a crepey effect resembling granite cloth. Also made in flecked, ribbed, diagonal, and brocade patterns and in silk, wool, and combinations. Similar to eponge. Tends to sag and stretch after washing. For skirts, suits, and dresses. Popular in the 1890s – 1950s; still on the market but under assorted names per the season's latest fashion label. See granite cloth, pages 46 and 110.

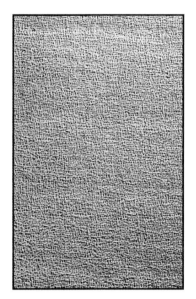

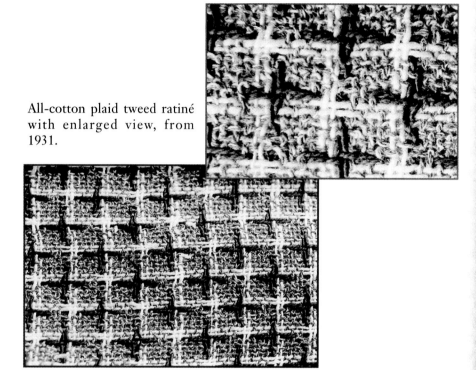

All-cotton plaid tweed ratiné with enlarged view, from 1931.

Late 1920s – early 1930s New Cloth, a Burton Bros. exclusive ratiné crepe with linen texture.

The many faces of Bontex ratiné and other crepe fabrics. *Pictorial Review*, May 1914.

Sateen, Satine

Satin, plain, or twill weaves; mercerized cotton; glossy, soft to touch, resembles real satin. True sateen has filling yarns on surface while Venetian types have warp yarns on surface. Some lining sateens are twill weave. Various grades for waist and skirt linings, bloomers, petticoats, draperies, comforters. See Venetian, page 88.

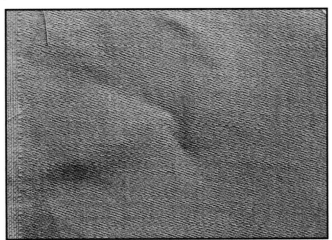

1930s fine dress and lining weight sateen.

Late 1940s – 1950s medium-weight drapery sateen with enlarged view; typical large floral print found on barkcloth, crash, and cretonne home décor fabrics so popular at that time.

Alaska Fibre garments used a heavy grade of sateen to cover and line cold-wear outer-clothing. *Ladies' Home Journal*, December 1896.

Sateen comforter. *Sears & Roebuck*, 1920. Courtesy Sears, Roebuck & Co.

Sateen apron dress and ratiné housedress made for the matronly figure. *Montgomery Ward*, 1925.

Sea Island Cotton

Plain weave; finest, longest staple cotton available, was grown off coast of Georgia (U. S. A.) but more recently in Brazil and the Carribean. Noted for its silkiness and luster, it is often described as the ultimate in pima taken to the next dimension. Still in use for lingerie, shirtings, slips, and fine garments.

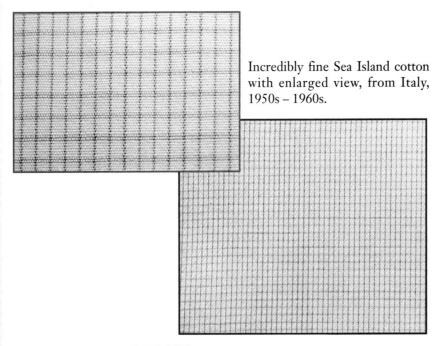

Incredibly fine Sea Island cotton with enlarged view, from Italy, 1950s – 1960s.

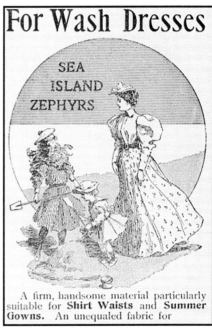

Sea Island Zephyrs were the best cottons according to this ad in *Ladies' Home Journal*, June 1896.

Fleeced-back Sea Island knit union suit. *Bellas Hess*, 1909.

Fashion in the field gets to the roots of a Sea Island plant in this 1908 school textbook. No hint as to height of the fastidious gent.

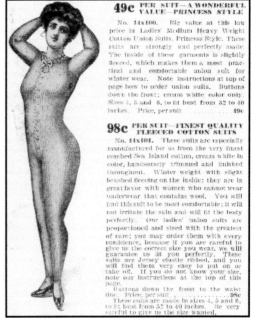

Seersucker

Plain weave, with alternating crinkled stripes made by holding alternate groups of warp yarns slack in the loom. Often mistaken for plissé. Name is a corruption of Persian shir-o-shakhar meaning milk and water; found in sixteenth century inventories and dictionaries; also cirsakas, eighteenth century. See "Fabric Identification by Appearance: The Look-alikes," page 128.

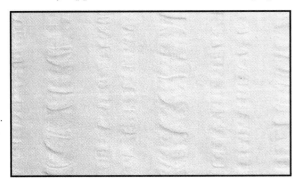

1910 ripple pleated seersucker voile from a summer skirt.

1930s medium weight seersucker often called bedspread dimity was the choice for warm-weather bed coverings.

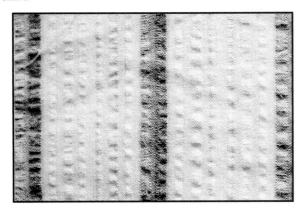

1940s – 1950s multicolored traditional striping; lightweight for loungewear or dress.

1950s traditional medium-weight summer suiting seersucker with enlarged view was trendy casual dress when coordinated with spectator shoes.

"Simplicity" Frock $2⁹⁸ [A]

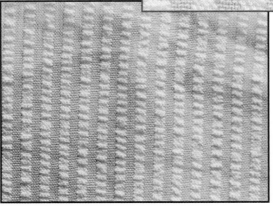

Seersucker housedresse, *National Bellas Hess*, 1946 – 1947.

Stifel Cloth and Other Indigoes

Umbrella name given to the various famous cottons, drills, calicoes, and indigo dyes produced by the Stifel Mfg. Co. from 1835 – 1957 when it was sold to Indian Head Mills. Two of the best-known brand names were Bulldog twilled shirtings and Miss Stifel Indigo Cloth. See "Fabric Identification by Width, Brand Names, Finishes, & Mills," page 151. Cloth discontinued in late 1950s though reproduction fabrics are available.

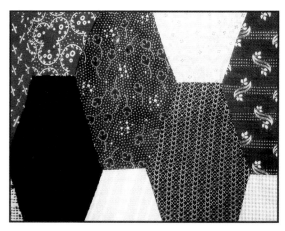

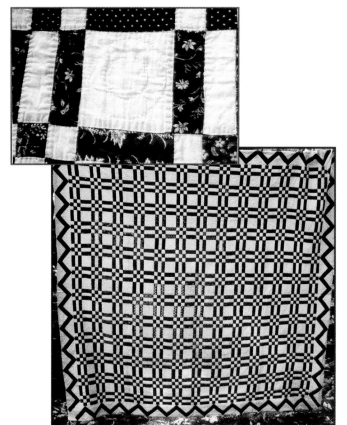

Indigo time capsule: 1830 indigo quilt with detailed section shows indigoes of that time compared to oblong one-patch quilt featuring indigoes of last-quarter nineteenth century. Sue Reich collection. Photos courtesy Sue Reich.

Indigo assortment from 1890 – 1910.

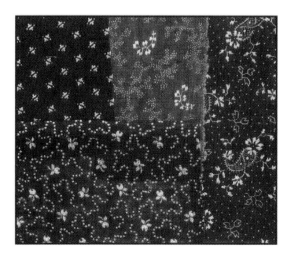

Sturdy Stifel indigo calico c. 1880 – 1900 with its famous boot logo stamped on reverse side. Leigh Fellner collection. Photo courtesy Leigh Fellner.

Stifel overalls of Miss Stifel Indigo Cloth featured in *McCall's Magazine*, December 1917. Shirley McElderry collection.

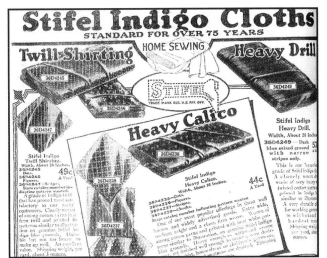

Stifel fabric selection. *Sears & Roebuck*, 1920. Courtesy Sears, Roebuck & Co.

Stifel sturdy work dress. *Charles Williams Stores*, 1927.

Tweed, Cotton

Plain, twill, or herringbone weaves woven to resemble homespun and rough, coarse, wiry, heavy wools.

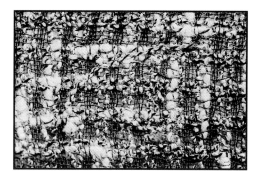

Sheer, nubby, lacy cotton tweed from 1931 has all the appearances and feel of its wool counterpart. See wool tweed, page 113.

Cotton tweed suit. *Chicago Mail Order Co.*, 1930.

Velveteen

Cotton version of velvet. See velvet listing in silk section for description, page 95.

Early 1900s embossed and solid velveteens with exceptional hand. Medium weight was adaptable for both skirts and capes.

Plain weave velveteen piqué from 1931. Wales are more rounded than corduroy making fabric drapable for lounging pajamas and suits.

Don't be Afraid
this is the
"A.W.B." Millerain

Velveteen and it is Rainproof. The water runs off of it like mercury, leaving no stain or dimmed lustre. Just the material for costumes and wraps.

Every woman needs just such a Rainproof, serviceable gown.

ASK FOR IT ANYWHERE

Millerain's waterproofed velveteen was ideal for outerwear shown in a *Ladies' Home Journal*, January 1895 ad.

Lustrous Velveteen Cape 3 B 721

$5⁹⁸

3B7

Fibre Wool Cre $5

Lustrous velveteen cape ensemble. *Bellas Hess & Co.*, 1922 – 1923.

Venetian

Satin weave with warp yarns on surface. Highly mercerized yarns on surface, heavier and superior to sateen. Same as farmers satin; not to be confused with Venetian cloth, a soft wool similar to wool broadcloth. Used for dresses, coat linings, and petticoats. Currently off-market by this name. See sateen, page 80.

1930s warp-face Venetian with enlarged view.

Venetian's luster and drapability shapes this dressy skirt called Nusatin. *Sears & Roebuck*, 1920. Courtesy Sears, Roebuck & Co.

Voile

Plain weave; soft, clinging thin transparent cloth made from gassed yarns, tightly twisted. Small mesh forms a perfect square making it easier to identify this from other sheers under a linen tester or magnifier. A fabric favorite dating back to eighteenth century. Often called gauze and mistaken for lawn and other semi-sheers. Softer, looser grades, such as curtain voile, are difficult to sew and snag easily. Also woven in silk, rayon, wool, and synthetics.

1918 – 1920 fancy clipspot Swiss voile with enlarged view. Fabric utilizes plain, mock leno and swivel weaves. See "Fabric Identification by Fiber, Weave, & Appearance" (page 127), for dotted Swiss information.

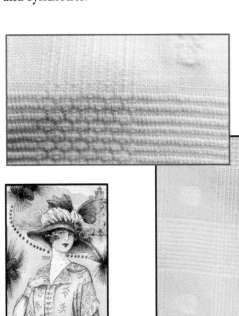

1930s colorful, sheer fine voile prints.

An indescribable embroidered voile creation. *Elite Styles*, October 1913.

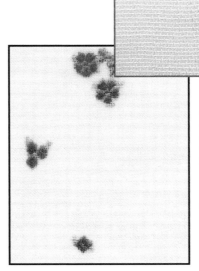

1950s elegant embroidered voile with enlarged view is an example of box loom. See "Fabric Identification by Fiber, Weave, & Appearance" (page 129), for dotted Swiss weaves.

Cotton and wool voile underskirts for cool weather warmth. *Bellas Hess & Co.*, 1909.

Nylon

First all-synthetic, nylon research began in 1927 and was completed in 1938; held off market until end of WWII. First pound made cost $27 million according to DuPont's research team. Nylon is a generic term for a large class of synthetic products, a multi-filament for textile yarns; monofilament for brushes, etc.; and plastics. The naming of the fiber went through several committee rounds for inventor Wallace Carothers, from Delawear, neosheen, Wacara norun, nuron, nulon, ni-lon, nee-lon, nigh-lon, and finally, nylon. As a fabric or blended with other fibers, nylon is durable and quick drying. Early nylon frayed and seams ripped easily; white yellowed quickly. See fiber chart in "Fabric Identification by Fiber, Weave, & Appearance," page 115, and brand names chart in "Fabric Identification by Width, Brand Names, Finishes, & Mills," page 136.

Mid-1950s floral nylon, a favorite for year-round loungewear and housecoats.

1950s reversible flocked-dot nylon for dresses or curtains.

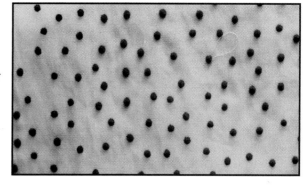

Nylon parachutes were a cheap fabric source for sewers for wedding gowns, curtains, linings, clothing, underwear, lampshades, and a host of other projects. *The Workbasket*, November 1948.

Nylon captured the blouse and tiered petticoat markets during the 1950s – early 1960s. *Montgomery Ward*, 1950 and 1957.

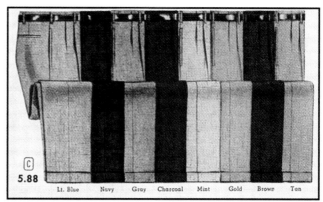

Dacron, the first polyester on the market, was often combined with nylon and popular for women's and men's clothing. *Montgomery Ward*, 1957.

Rayon and Acetate

Called artificial silk or art silk prior to 1924, rayon has become as popular if not more so than silk. Generic term for rayon filaments is regenerated cellulose and is made from cellulose by either viscose or cuppramonium process. Rayon can be blended with any fiber to add elegance, swish, drape, weightiness, luster and great hand to any fabric – name a fabric and there is most likely a rayon version of it. Acetate is a modified rayon fiber and has its own fiber classification. See "Fabric Identification by Fiber, Weave, and Appearance," rayon fibers and "Fabric Identification by Width, Brand Names, Finishes, & Mills," brand names sections for history of this filament.

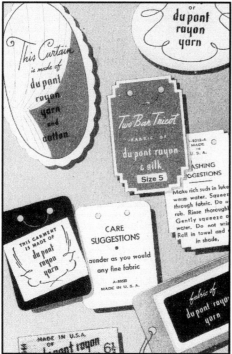

Rayon reigned during the 1930s through 1950s — an assortment of rayon fashions and fabrics for every occasion and their care from 1930 *Chicago Mail Order Co.*, *National Bellas Hess*, 1946 (note Ara-fab dress, see Aralac listing), and DuPont labels from *Facts About Fabrics* rayon booklet c. 1950. Courtesy E.I. Du Pont de Nemours and Company.

Aralac

One of the earliest of fibers developed from milk protein, aralac was blended with rayon to create a substitute wool. It appeared on the market around 1940 and during WWII replaced the manufacture of new wool for civilian clothing. Soft, warm, and with all the features of wool, its main drawback was smelling like sour milk when wet. The fabric never really caught on, and became obsolete around 1948 as it couldn't compete with the new post-war synthetics.

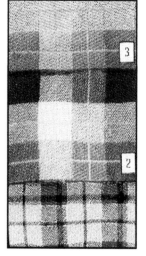

An array of aralac fabrics, a blend of protein and rayon, used as a wool substitute during WWII. *Sears & Roebuck*, 1943. Courtesy Sears, Roebuck & Co. See "Fabric Identification by Fiber, Weave, and Appearance," rayon fibers, page 123.

Brocade

Is a specific name to the seventeenth and eighteenth centuries. From Spanish, *brodaco*, Italian, *brocaddo*, English, *broach/brooch*, all words deriving from cloth of gold and silver, bossed or embossed as in nails and studs. Cloth is a jacquard weave and often called jacquard. Pattern can be on satin or twill background in self or contrasting color raised on cloth. Brocade has a more embossed appearance while damask has a flat effect.

See brocade in "Fabric Identification by Fiber, Weave, and Appearance," jacquard weave section, page 127.

Crepe

Is a broad range of fabrics having a fancy weave formed during weaving or by chemical application after weaving to create diverse crinkled or grained surface effects on cottons, silks, wools, rayons, and synthetics. Fabric is made from highly twisted yarns ranging from fine flat to pebbly and mossy textures. Crepe has been popular for all fashions since its development in sixteenth century Bologna. Some notable crepes are crepe de chine, de laine, Georgette, lisseé, messaline, romaine, and crepe-back satin.

Flat crepes have barely discernible texture and were often inaccurately called French crepes. Floral patterns like All-tyme Crepe Brand from 1942 were very popular into the mid-1950s for loungewear and pajamas. Washable but must be ironed wet to remove wrinkles.

Comfortably, slinky rayon loungewear. *Chicago Mail Order Co.*, 1934.

Moiré
See description in silk section, page 101.

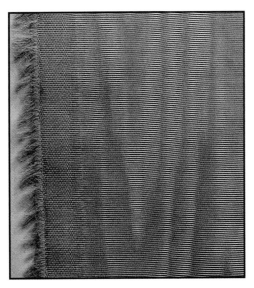

1950s wide-patterned acetate moirés were adaptable to formal wear as well as home decorating.

Taffeta
See description in silk section, page 105.

Rayon taffeta bedroom ensemble. *National Bellas Hess*, 1937.

Glamorous formals of rayon taffeta covered by rayon net overskirts. *Montgomery Ward*, 1950.

Silk

Silk was called *sse*, the heavenly insect, by the Chinese who were first to reel this protein filament from the silkworm in 2640 BCE. Its manufacturing process was kept secret for nearly 3,500 years before traders in the Middle East and Asia deviously gained access to sericulture. The production of silk is labor intensive making it costly for consumers who value this fabric's beauty and luster and will willingly pay the price. Other names for silk: Greek, *serikon*, Latin, *sericum*, Italian, *seta*, Spanish, *ceda*, French, *soie*, German, *Seide*, Korean, *sir*, and Russian, *sheolk*.

A variety of silk styles from fluttery sheers to soft flat crepe to rustling taffeta to shimmery charmeuse — gowns for admiring at Delmonico's perhaps and possibly fashioned from silks of the highly esteemed Cheney Silk Co. *Elite Styles*, October 1913. Dressy for stepping out, *Charles Williams Stores Inc.*, 1927.

Silks and velvets of many types make up this 1890s crazy quilt made by a child. Pat Cummings collection. Photo courtesy James Cummings.

Brocade and Fancies
See rayon section for description, page 93.

Early 1900s silk brocade with equally desirable sides.

A fancy assortment of brocades and dobbies from 1890s to WWI.

The LaDue family of Nelsonville, New York used silk brocades, velvets and ornate embellishings of ribbons, handpainting and appliqués to make this crazy quilt, c. 1880s – 1890s. Dana Balsamo collection. Photo courtesy Dana Balsamo.

Chantilly Lace

Chantilly lace derives its name from Chantilly, France where it was created during the seventeenth century and has been popular since as a dress fabric and a fine lace trim. Its beauty lies in the dull grenadine silk used for the fine net double ground and delicate patterns and the contrasting heavier cordonnet yarn to outline patterns. Originally made of white linen or silk, chantilly is also available today in nylon and other fibers.

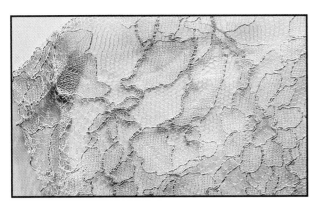

1930s silk chantilly lace yardage from France with its distinct corded outlines was *de rigueur* for social events.

Chantilly was one of several laces recommended for this costume. *Ladies' Home Journal*, June 1891.

China Silk

Plain weave; originally a fine-quality, hand-woven silk from China or Japan. Due to rising costs, commercial china silk of an inferior quality appeared around the 1890s. Fabric was used then as it is today for linings and children's wear.

Early 1900s better grade china silk is not as wispy as those currently on the market.

Marie Antoinette summer costume of printed china silk. *Ladies' Home Journal*, May 1895.

Crepe
See rayon section for description, page 93.

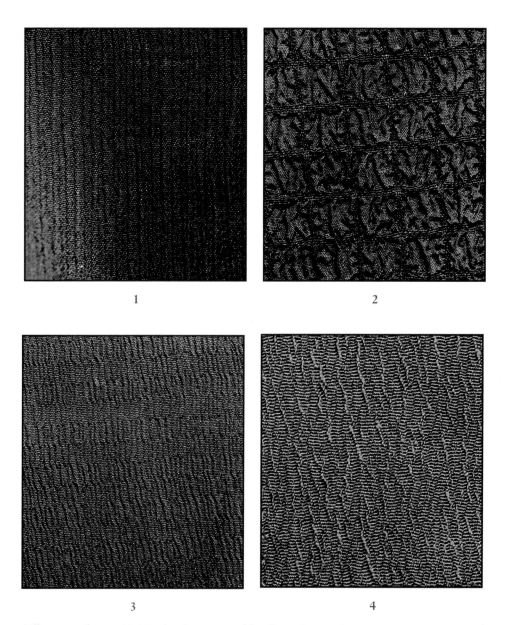

Silk crepes from 1935 Butler Bros. swatchbook: 1. Serpentine or waterweave grooved with a woven-in wavy, crinkly stripe; weighted; preshrunk; washable; 2. Matelassé, woven quilted or padded surface, weighted, washable; 3. Ruff (rough) medium to deep-loomed texture; also called cloqué; weighted. Ruff appears to be a fashion term particular to the 1930s; 4. Trebark (tree bark) so named as it resembles the rough bark on trees and has the most extreme surface interest of all the crepes. Texture is woven in and guaranteed to be permanent.

The many faces of silk crepes — Georgette dress and blouses. *Sears & Roebuck*, 1920. Courtesy Sears, Roebuck & Co. and *Chicago Mail Order Co.*, 1930. Canton crepe dress. *Bellas Hess & Co.*, 1922. Lingerie, *Chicago Mail Order Co.*, 1934.

Faille

Plain weave; soft, flat horizontal rib, wider and flatter than grosgrain but narrower and not as pronounced as bengaline or ottoman. An old fabric dating to at least first quarter nineteenth century and an especially prominent dress fabric in the 1850s – 1860s. Vertical ribbing fashionable in late 1940s – 1950s. Also see taffeta, page 105.

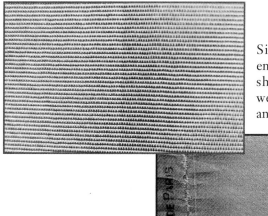

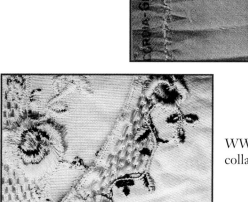

Silk faille assortment with enlarged view – 1930s Concardia showing damage from heavy weighting, 1940s baby fine rib and WWI ombre tones.

WWI silk faille narrow shawl-type collar with silk embroidery.

Late 1870s – early 1880s sleeveless silk faille basque; beads serve as sleeves and give a cape effect to garment. Judith Scoggin Gridley collection.

Moiré

French meaning watered; preferred fabric is taffeta, faille, or cotton. Original finish was produced by folding cloth lengthwise, face in and pressing with moisture and heat. This produced a natural water effect in a design which was repeated on either side of the center. Tabine taffeta in the seventeenth century was moiréd and enhanced with gold threads. Today, engraved rollers produce designs although finish is not permanent.

1930 various silk moiré patterns possibly from men's ties.

Rubberized silk moiré and other fine silk rainwear. *Bellas Hess*, 1909.

Mousseline De Soie, Silk Organdy or Silk Muslin

Plain weave; soft fabric usually finished with a light sizing for body but still softer than today's organza. By 1920s had been mostly replaced by organza as it did not launder well and had little longevity. The mousseline family includes mousseline, mousseline matte, mousseline satin, and mousseline de laine. See listing under wool, page 108.

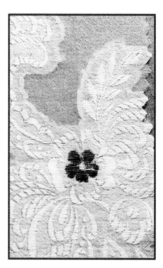

Edwardian silk organdy with embroidered and metallic motifs.

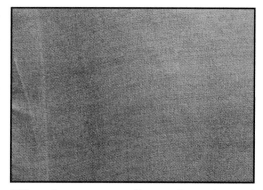

Silk satin organza or l'organdie satiné and sometimes known as ziberline is a favorite for bridal wear. Surface sheen comes from its filling-face satin weave.

Organza

Seventeenth century Italian *organzino* or *organzine*, a special type of strong silk thread. Of plain weave, the modern version patented by an Italian designer in the 1950s as L'organza is wirier and crisper and was made to flatter 1950s fashions.

Ottoman

Plain weave, usually a heavy corded silk, rayon or nylon fabric with cotton cord filling. Broad filling ribs alternate with smaller ribs. Sometimes referred to as fat, fancy faille.

Early 1900s medium-weight silk ottoman.

Early 1900s silk pongee; Japanese stamp is proof that inspection meets U.S. government import standards for quality.

Pongee

From Chinese *pen-chi* meaning "home loom" or "woven at home." Name for a wide variety of silk cloths from northern China. The oak-leaf silkworm produces pongee, shantung, hohan, antung, and ninghai. Plain weave with a hint of texture from finer warp than filling or ribbing; similar to silk broadcloth, poplin, and a finer version of shantung. Usually left in its original ecru or natural color.

Satin

Its satin weave gives this ever-popular, lustrous, drapable silk its name. Dates to the Middle Ages where it originated in Zaytoun (Zaitin, Canton), China. When satin arrived in Europe in the twelfth – thirteenth centuries the spelling was aceytuin and in Italy, zetain. From the original Chinese spelling the term was contracted to zetin, finally to satin. By the fourteenth century, satin was the court favorite in England. Satin comes in many weights and styles, each nuance assigned its own name – satin de chine, de Lyons, Duchesse, Turc, Serrano, panne, messaline, Merveilleux, luxor, Empresse, deBurges, crepe, Gree, alcyonne, deChypre and canton are but a few. Also made in cotton (sateen, satine, satinette) and synthetics. Uses range from clothing to home décor.

1920s – 1930s cotton-back silk lining used in men's coats and vests. Often called Merveilleux after a high-quality brand name silk lining.

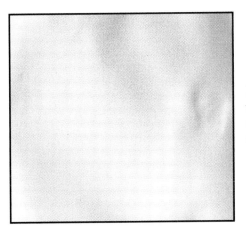

Lustrous 1950s silk satin in a rich, heavier weight known as bridal, slipper, duchess, or satin duchess. Judith Scoggin Gridley collection.

Silk satin for stompin' at the Savoy. *Chicago Mail Order Co.*, 1930 – 1931.

Serge

Twill weave; same as surah but heavier with more pronounced twill. Also made in various grades of wool dating back to sixteenth century of nearly every fabric made in black or blue piece dye including 7-oz. storm serge for ladies' wear. Used for outer garments, linings, and facings.

1930s fancy stripe silk serge with enlarged view.

Surah

Originated in Surat, northwestern India and taken to France for manufacturing. Soft silk, fine twill weave. Types include chevron, herringbone pattern; ecossais quadrille is a tartan effect; gros cole is a heavy, closely woven thick silk with lustrous finish on both sides.

1940s silk surah with enlarged view.

Taffeta

From Persian *taftah*, silken cloth derived from verb taftan — to shine, twist, spin; spelled taffata in mid-fourteenth century English; old French, tapheta. Plain weave closely woven; is silk counterpart of finest cotton percales and pimas. Among the many types of taffetas from fifteenth century – eighteenth century were caffa and capha, heavy, coarse; sarcenet, thin for linings; tupelo, tufted with stripes of velvet; and Spanish taffeta. From 1890s through 1930 taffetas split more readily due to abusive heavy tin weighting to increase body and rustle or scroop as demanded by public at that time.

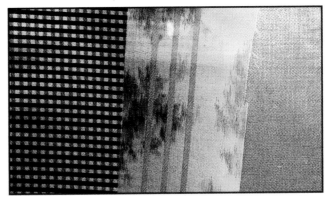

Silk taffeta assortment — early 1900s tissue-weight check, WWI – 1920s woven warp print with satin weave striping and 1950s iridescent shot.

An elaborate Civil War gown worn to a tea party hosted by Mrs. Lincoln at the White House. Fabric was ordered from Paris for the occasion. Dawna Ellenberger and Old Mill Village Museum collection. Photo courtesy Linda Learn.

Edwardian refinement in silk taffeta. *Bellas Hess*, 1909.

Silk taffeta petticoats for silk taffeta gowns. *Bellas Hess*, 1909.

Velvet

From Latin *vilus* or *velvetum* denoting shaggy hair; Old English *veluett* or *veluet* c. 1320; Italian *velluto*; Old French *velut*; Spanish and Portugese *velludo*. Plain, twill or satin weaves; broad and elusive term covers all warp pile fabrics except terry and plush which are created by shearing loop piles. Some silk velvets have silk pile and backs but most silk velvets have rayon or cotton backs. Velvet woven also in rayon and nylon and combinations. Velvets in the sixteenth century represented a variety of patterns from checkered, changeable, figured, mottled, double pile called velvet upon velvet, unshorn with loops uncut and wrought which was decorated with embroidery. Those who could not afford velvet wore a look-alike called mocado, a wool pile with linen backing which came in stripes, plain and tufted, and reportedly Queen Elizabeth had several dresses of this fabric in her wardrobe.

1920s plain weave, fancy-cut pile mohair and silk velvet which once was a covering for a piano stool. Linda Learn collection.

Gorgeous hat creations in silk velvet. *Sears & Roebuck*, 1920. Courtesy Sears, Roebuck & Co.

Wool

Generally the textile and fashion fields regard wool, a protein fiber, as a product of domesticated sheep, placing vicuna, llama, goats, camel, and alpacas in a group called specialty hairs. Sheep have been domesticated for about 8,000 years for food and about 6,000 years for clothmaking. Records and seals have been found for making wool garments in Babylonia in 4000 BCE, and it was a thriving industry in Rome around 80 CE. Wool, which is derived from the Old English *wull*, is revered for its excellent insulation, versatility, resilience, and beauty. The following wool terms, which date well back into the 1600s – 1700s, are still around today and used in a very general sense for any wool wovens, sometimes interchangeably: cloth – warp and filling spun from carded wool; stuff – warp and filling spun from combed wool; and serge – carded filling, warped combed.

Luxurious wool for snuggly warmth — wool felt slippers. *Sears & Roebuck*, 1920. Courtesy Sears, Roebuck & Co. Wool felt chapeaus. *Chicago Mail Order Co.*, 1930. Colorful jacquard blankets. *Montgomery Ward*, 1939.

Batiste
Plain weave, fine semi-sheer, similar to voile and nun's veiling. See cotton batiste, page 10, for history.

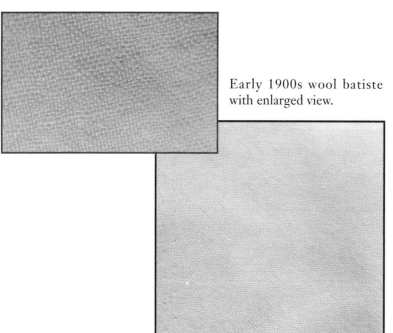

Early 1900s wool batiste with enlarged view.

Sheer and lightweight wools such as batiste, challis, crepe, and voile created the perfect drape for these styles. *Farm and Home*, September 1922.

Challis and Mousseline de Laine (muslin wool)
Plain and twill weaves; semi-sheer; characterized by cotton warp, wool double filling yarns. Mousseline de Laine name shortened to delaine in late 1880s and at some unknown point merged with challis. Fabrics similar to batiste.

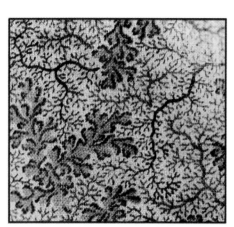

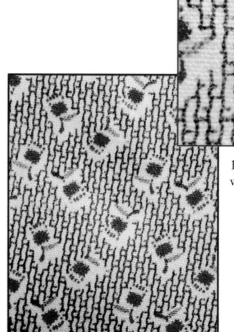

1920s wool and silk challis with enlarged view.

1850s twill weave mousseline de laine from a dress of that era. See percale listing, page 67, for lining from this dress.

Flannel

Plain and twill weave, light to medium weight, soft with slight nap. According to an 1883 Draper's Dictionary, the name probably came from gwlanen (still the Welsh name for the material in 1883), which denotes simply woolen. Terms used in the Middle Ages were flanella and flannen. Flannel had supposedly been the principal textile product of Wales where fairs were commonly held solely for the selling of flannels. Drapers describe flannels as made of woolen yarn, slightly twisted in the spinning, and of open texture, the objective to have the cloth soft and spongy without regard to strength. Flannels which have pile raised on one side (done by teasels or by cards and called perching) are termed raised flannels; when both sides are so covered they are double-raised flannels. There are also milled and double-milled flannels.

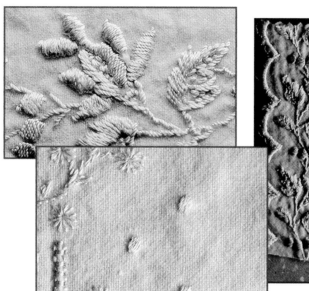

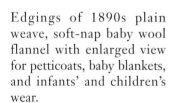

Edgings of 1890s plain weave, soft-nap baby wool flannel with enlarged view for petticoats, baby blankets, and infants' and children's wear.

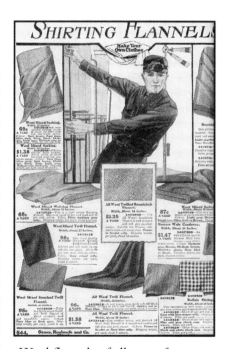

Wool flannels of all types for every occasion. *Sears & Roebuck*, 1920. Courtesy Sears, Roebuck & Co.

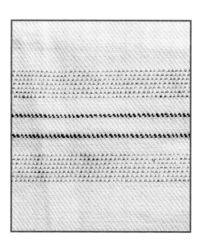

Circa WWI twill weave wool flannel, flat nap, lightweight for dresses. This is similar today to a revival of a cotton called Swiss flannel.

Wool flannel suit and coat ensembles were post-WWII important fashion statements. *National Bellas Hess*, 1946 – 1947.

Gabardine

English translation of the Spanish word *gabardina*, meaning Mackintosh or raincoat. Originally a water-proofed fabric like serge or Rigby Cloth. Twill weave, worsted fabric similar to whipcord; finish either hard and smooth like worsted or dull and soft like woolens.

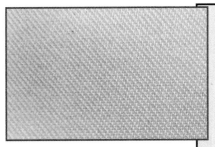

A family affair — home-tailored wool gabardine suit and enlarged view; woolen mill's label was supplied with each purchase of yardage. Suit was made by Jessey Scoggin for her daughter-in-law Audrey Scoggin, who passed it on to her daughter Judith, who passed it on to her daughter Jessie, shown modeling suit. Although given much service over 50 years, suit is still in prime condition and wearable, the circular skirt still holding alignment of no-sag seams and hem. Judith Scoggin Gridley collection.

Granite Cloth

Fancy crepe weave, see definition in cotton section, page 46. Currently off-market by this name.

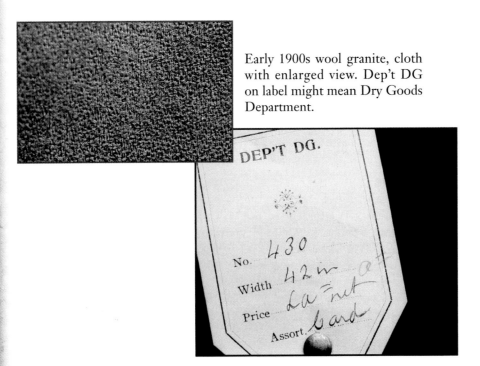

Early 1900s wool granite, cloth with enlarged view. Dep't DG on label might mean Dry Goods Department.

Wool and wool blend dress crepes were lightweight yet warm. *McCall's Magazine*, November 1904. Also see granite listing in cotton section, page 46.

Hugenot Sacking

Plain weave which resembles weave structure of feedsacking and hopsacking and probably from which its name derives. Resembles medium-grade flannel and is soft and feathery to the touch. Name may be regional or used among tradesmen as it doesn't appear in major vintage and modern textile dictionaries or glossaries.

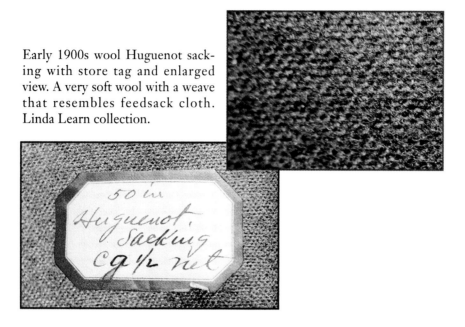

Early 1900s wool Huguenot sacking with store tag and enlarged view. A very soft wool with a weave that resembles feedsack cloth. Linda Learn collection.

Overcoating

Various weaves. An overall term for heavy, durable wools which were used for outer wear, usually men's garments. Fabrics ranged from solids to textures to fancy patterns.

Early 1900s fancy-striped wool twill overcoating with enlarged view is heavy enough for arctic blasts.

The latest in wool overcoatings for the gent of fine taste. *Ladies' Home Journal*, October 1895.

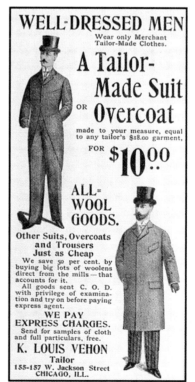

Suiting

Like overcoating, skirting and shirting suiting is a general classification for wools, rayons, cottons, and silks, or combinations of those fibers in fancy weaves, textures, and patterns. Usually fabric was a blend involving cotton and of a weight preferable for spring or fall, although not limited to those seasons.

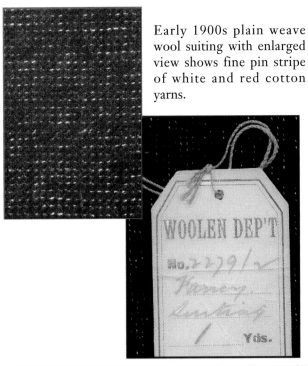

Early 1900s plain weave wool suiting with enlarged view shows fine pin stripe of white and red cotton yarns.

Two Handsome Fall and Winter Costumes

From Our New 64-Page Catalogue

118 Other Beautiful Styles Also Illustrated and Described

All our materials are new and include the latest importations—"NORMANDIE" and "VICTORIA" suitings shown only by us.

A TRIAL ORDER COSTS YOU NOTHING
As we REFUND YOUR MONEY if we fail to please you. It is very important to us, therefore, that we should make your garment right; otherwise the loss is ours.

EVERYTHING MADE TO ORDER—NOTHING READY-MADE
200,000 satisfied customers prove the success of our system

Our catalogue fully explains the quick, easy and economical way whereby you may have a fashionable garment made to your measure and not risk a dollar. Is it worth while to bother with dressmakers and go on tiresome shopping expeditions, when you have only to select your style and material in your own home, mail us your order, and in less than ten days receive a perfectly satisfactory garment?

Prices lower than ever before

Tailor-Made Suits, - - $10 to $25	Fall and Winter Jackets, $10 to $20
New "Lohengrin" Suits, - $15 to $25	Long Coats, "Tourist Models" $12 to $20
Skirts of Exclusive Design, $ 4 to $12	Rain Coats, - - - - $12 to $20

We Prepay Express Charges on any garment you purchase from us, to any part of the United States

Our prices are low and we will tell you why. We purchase our Materials in immense quantities and sell at wholesale prices direct to our customers, thereby saving them the retailer's profit.

FREE Our New Fall and Winter Catalogue and a fine assortment of samples of our latest materials, will be sent free to any part of the United States. Kindly state whether you wish samples for a suit, skirt or cloak, and about the colors you prefer, and be sure to ask for Catalogue No. 53. They will be sent by return mail.

NATIONAL CLOAK & SUIT COMPANY, 119 and 121 West 23d St., New York City

Mail Orders Only   ESTABLISHED 16 YEARS   No Agents or Branches

Wool suitings for fashion-plate ladies. *McCall's Magazine*, November 1904.

Cosmopolitan men's wool suits in a variety of textures. *Chicago Mail Order Co.*, 1930.

Tweed

Plain or twill, usually rough textured. Can be woven with mixture of various types of wool strains. Sometimes blended with cotton or silk. Name coined by an error in 1831 when someone mistook the Scottish word tweel (twill) for tweed. Not named after the River Tweed in Scotland! Galashiels, Jedburgh, and Hawick were large producers of tweeds.

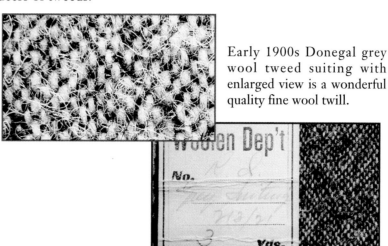

Early 1900s Donegal grey wool tweed suiting with enlarged view is a wonderful quality fine wool twill.

1940s handsome Irish wool tweed in soft heathery tones with enlarged view.

Wool tweeds for sporty knickers. *Charles Williams Stores*, 1927. And for dressy suits. *Chicago Mail Order Co.*, 1930.

Zibeline
Plain weave; heavy woolen coating with long, shaggy nap laid in one direction. Never goes out of fashion.

Fall 1904 wool panne (or panné) zibeline with enlarged view. Panne indicates that the fabric's usually long nap was pressed flat to increase sheen.

Sumptuous zibeline with a dash of fur. *Sears & Roebuck*, 1920. Courtesy Sears, Roebuck & Co.

Buying, Pricing, and Thread Count

What to Look for and What to Avoid

Aside from big house auction reports on valuable textile sales, there appear to be no catalogs or other perennial sources listing prices of common vintage fabrics per se. Unlike dolls, paintings, glass and chinaware, and furniture, for example, which have periodically published price guides, the person attempting to find prices for everyday old fabrics has no such resource documentation. To some extent, online auction sales and publications on collectible and antique clothing have filled this void as a means to establish prices.

In attempting to present a price guideline in the broadest sense, the authors felt that a marketplace without regional boundaries and which would be readily available to the average collector and user anywhere would be most representative for obtaining price ranges.

The obvious choice was the Internet. Selected and surveyed were vintage fabric website dealers who are established, recognized, reputable, and knowledgeable in their field, and who offer goods in prime condition. Online auctions, auction houses, flea markets, regional stores, quilt shows, doll shows, textile shows, and the like were not considered for one or more of the following: fabrics not within our timeframe; seller uncertainty about fiber, fabric name or estimated date; insufficient information about fabric; insufficient selection of fabrics such as wool and nylon; and domination of specialty, rare, and valuable fabrics seldom available and appealing only to institutions and high rollers and not within the average person's wish list or pocketbook.

As you read prices listed here, keep in mind they represent, at best, a price range for cloth in excellent to good condition without blemish or damage. It was observed in our surveying that used cloth, such as quilt backings and drapes and slightly soiled cloth, sell for about 30 to 40 percent less than if perfect, and that scrap bags are priced very reasonably. It should also be noted that manufacturers' and salesmen's swatch cards and samplebooks, which bring premium prices due to scarcity, are not included as part of this price list. Also not included are yardage with labels, stampings, brand names in selvages and provenance such as sales slips, which are added bonuses and which can command slightly higher prices. It is difficult to provide estimates for these less frequently available goods which can fluctuate according to buyer response at the time of sale.

All in all, this price guide is intended to help the prospective buyer be aware of the current market prices of common, everyday vintage fabrics and to serve as an aid when bidding and buying or pricing for sale. Prices are given for the yard unless otherwise noted. Brand names are capitalized to denote trademark or registration.

Fiber	What to Look for and What to Avoid	Price
Cotton and linens pre-1880 Yardage available but limited; other sources: cut-up clothing, bedding, household items and remnants. Prime survivors: calico, cambric, challis, cheviot, chintz, cretonne, gauze, gingham, homespun types, muslin, linen, osnaburg, and voile/gauzes.	These fabrics are in particular demand by quilters, costumers, and study/research groups. Most fabrics can be obtained from website dealers, specialty antique stores, and textile and quilting shows. Many fabrics are not colorfast and may show signs of fading and aging, particularly if fabric is reused, such as a quilt backing. Ask for seller's written authentication for age; add condition if from online purchase. Avoid if there are any doubts or fabric is damaged beyond your intended use.	Demand and rarity can command high prices. $70.00 – $125.00; indigo, $95.00.

Fiber	What to Look for and What to Avoid	Price
Cotton and linens 1880 – 1919 Larger selection available especially batiste, calicoes, challis, chambray, conversation prints, fancies/novelties, fine plains, gauzes, gingham, lawns, linen, muslins, percales, quilter's shirtings, sateens.	Follow same inspection steps as for pre-1880 and time periods which follow in the next age groups. Dyes for the most part are not colorfast; verify gingham is authentic — ginghams are woven, imitation or print ginghams are printed check or plaid patterns and found mostly on percales and muslins. Verify fabrics are as advertised — linen, not cotton; cotton, not poly blend, silk, not rayon, etc. See pages 121 – 131 for burn tests and look-alikes. Feel flocked dots on dotted Swiss – paste or composition appear in early 1900s – 1930s; plastic and painted 1940s or later. Avoid suspicious advertising or sales pitches.	**1880s** – $65.00 – $96.00 overall; indigo $65.00 – $85.00; mourning prints $40.00; most fabrics 24" wide. **1890** – $52.00 – $94.00 overall, with most in $66.00 – $76.00 range; shirting $20.00 – $35.00; chintz, $94.00; velvet $25.00 plain – $85.00 figural. **1900 – 1919** – $22.00 – $45.00 with most in $25.00 – $30.00 range; ginghams $20.00 – $30.00; homespuns $45.00.

Fiber	What to Look for and What to Avoid	Price
Cotton and linens 1920 – 1939 Good assortment of staple cottons, barkcloth, feedsacks, plissé, seersucker, selvage stampings, sheers, whimsical and novelty prints are available. Especially desirable: 1920 – 1930s Art Deco prints, textured linen, gauzy muslin, plissé, ripple-cloths such as Kimono Cloth and Ripplette, whimsical prints, Mexican topical prints, barkcloth, oilcloth, feedsacks, Indian Head, Cloth of Gold, Quadriga Cloth and E&W, ABC, Peter Pan, Soisette, Flaxon.	Follow previous inspection tips. Look for large stitches in feedsacks or large stitch holes on opened sacks to verify authenticity. Solid colors are in demand; look for signs of dyeing; seams will be same color as sack if dyed by other than manufacturer. Feedsacks are a special category; be especially well informed before you buy. Check oilcloth texture; it will be slightly grainier or less slick than plastic and vinyl imitations and probably have signs of cracking or splitting. Look for Indian Head, Cloth of Gold, and E&W Quadriga Cloth and other brand names in selvage; if they are advertised as not showing selvage markings, get written verification and photo of selvage from seller. Quadriga is needleized; under magnifier or linen tester surface will reveal microholes.	$7.00 – $50.00 overall; chintz $16.00 – $50.00; dimity $14.00; dotted Swiss $7.00 – $13.00; florals $25.00 – $45.00; geometrics $10.00 – $20.00. gingham (which is in abundance) $14.00 – $20.00; lawn $14.00 – $25.00; poplin $14.00; shirting $18.00 – $30.00. For special categories and feedsacks, see next time period.

Fiber	What to Look for and What to Avoid	Price
Cotton and linens 1940 – 1959 Good selection including flocked cottons. Especially desirable: flocked patterns, iridescent chambray, metallic prints, Moygashel linen, novelty piqués and cloqués (deeply textured ridges or ripples) and novelty, floral, and thematic prints.	Continue with previous tips, dyes are more stabilized, colorfast and washfast. Barkcloth was at its peak; know difference between simulated and genuine barkcloth – barkcloth will be textured, simulated will be smooth surface. Examine for textures which can be large striations or allover tiny pebbly or blistered grains to resemble bark. Cloth was made in cotton and rayon/cotton blend or all rayon in 1940s – 1950s and Fiberglas in late 1950s – 1960s. Beware of advertised cottons which are actually blended with rayon, Dacron or other early synthetics. See burn test chart in "Fabric Identification by Fiber, Weave, & Appearance," page 123, or get written verification from seller. Beware butcher linen (not butcher's linen) which is a rayon/cotton that resembles linen; fabric unstable, stretches lengthwise, shrinks widthwise.	$10.00 – $34.00 overall, except for specialty categories and feedsacks which are listed separately; border prints $12.00 – $22.00; calico and calico types (most likely percale) $12.00 – $28.00; chambray $25.00; chintz $9.00 standard $25.00 – $55.00 special; dimity $12.00 – $14.00; dotted Swiss (including flocked) $10.00 – $16.00; flannelette $8.00 – $25.00; geometrics and prints $10.00 – $28.00; gingham $12.00 – $16.00; Indian Head $8.00 – $15.00; metallics $12.00; organdy $12.00 – $16.00; paisleys $16.00; percale $10.00; plissé $16.00; piqué $10.00 – $16.00; sateen $8.00 – $9.00; voile $12.00 – $16.00. **Specialty categories:** animal and toy prints $24.00 – $34.00; barkcloth $22.00 – $70.00 (sold mostly by the piece); florals and fruits $10.00 – $32.00; home décor fabrics $16.00 – $25.00 (sold mostly by the piece); juvenile prints $40.00 – $92.00, as low as $20.00 for more common designs; novelty prints $20.00 – $70.00 with most in $35.00 – $40.00 range; thematics (such as sports and western) $20.00 – $32.00. **Feedsacks:** 1930s – 1940s – 1950s border $15.00 – $38.00; checks $10.00; prints, geometrics, and florals $12.00 – $42.00; novelty and scenics $30.00 – $100.00 (most in $40.00 range); solids $37.00 – $45.00; whimsies $30.00. For comparison, online opening bids average $15.00.

Fiber	What to Look for and What to Avoid	Price
Nylon and Dacron 1940 – 1959	If you are considering adding nylon and first-generation synthetics such as Dacron to your collection, get fiber verification or, if you have a microscope, ask for a swatch to test and do a burn test as described in "Fabric Identification by Fiber, Weave, & Appearance," page 123. Sheer polys are often mistaken for nylon. Early nylon frays easily and yellowed whites are difficult to restore. Most vintage nylons, excluding net and tulle, are found in dotted Swiss kitchen curtains and children's confirmation dresses.	No price range due to insufficient listings and lack of information (including a survey of online auctions).

Fiber	What to Look for and What to Avoid	Price
Rayon mid-1920s – 1959 Limited selection found. It is helpful if you understand crepe types so you know what you have purchased. Vintage rayons were termed flat, moss, pebble, and ruff, with each crepe more textured. Your fingertips are a handy guide for distinguishing.	Most rayons are washable before sewing, but may need to be drycleaned afterwards. Washables need to be ironed wet; most fray easily. Get as much information as possible from seller.	Brocade $11.00 overall; blends with cotton $16.00; prints (not known if flat or crepe), $10.00 – $30.00. Usually sold by the piece.

Fiber	What to Look for and What to Avoid	Price
Silk, any era Extremely limited selection of 1930s – 1950s silks available. Especially desirable: all-silk velvet, iridescent taffetas, faille, brocades, dobbies, fancies, designer prints, kimono silk.	Continue with previous tips. Beware old silk through 1930s which has been weighted, particularly taffeta and brocade. Check for hidden splitting and avoid if splits are found as it will be indicative of most of fabric's condition. Get written verification that advertised silk is not rayon or a blend. Also see "Fabric Identification by Fiber, Weave, & Appearance," page 123, for burn test chart.	Prints (unknown if flat or crepe) $14.00 – $45.00 with most in the $27.00 – $30.00 range; taffeta $16.00. Specialty, high-end silks: dupioni $100.00; jacquard $400.00; shantung $350.00 – $400.00.

Fiber	What to Look for and What to Avoid	Price
Wool, any era Wool is difficult to protect from pest damage and odor can be difficult to remove. Especially desirable: Viyella, Harris tweed, batiste, voile, challis, mousseline de laine, linsey-woolsey and home-spuns.	Continue with previous tips. Check for moth holes and other pest damage to which wool is extremely susceptible; avoid if extensive damage. Avoid if mustiness or other strong odors are detected. Get written verification that advertised wool is not a blend or what blend is — cotton, silk, or linen which were favorite fiber combos in old wools, and Acrilan in late 1950s.	No price range due to insufficient listings and lack of information.

Buying Tips – Ask, Examine, Repeat Three Times

It's buyer beware, and those words of warning should be sufficient to make you cautious and inquisitive.

Know Your Seller

Ask, ask, ask to get feel for seller's knowledge and sincerity; absolutely essential if you are buying online. Check feedback on auction sites and get verification from seller if fabric is unfamiliar to you, or if label or description do not match your conception of a fabric's name or appearance. Ask for a swatch or more detailed verification and a return guarantee whether purchase is made online or in person.

Examine, Examine, Examine

If fabric is a garment, lay out full length to check for pinholes, rust spots, stains, insect infestation or damage, browning, yellowing, color runs, off-grain printing, moth holes, odor and perspiration stains, or other imperfections. Rust spots denote fiber rot and seldom can be removed successfully without leaving holes. Browning, yellowing, and other minor discolorations can be washed out, but faint traces may be left after laundering. Off-grain printing can't be straightened, crocking can't be cured, splitting and worn areas warn of danger ahead. Touch, feel, poke; tug to test for thin, worn areas and on silk for splitting; run hand over or rub fabric together for crocking (dyes which rub off). Check if fabric is in original condition or has been laundered. Eyeball thread count and quality. Better yet, carry a linen tester to reveal type of and condition of weave structure. Ask about previous storage conditions if fabric smells; odors and mildew can be difficult to remove, some will remain. Moth holes and insect damage require serious consideration as not all damage is visible. Merchandise advertised as from a non-smoking home or environment may mean only the current environment and not previous locations, which may not have been free from smoke and other damaging fumes. Consider how important damage is for your purposes. Many imperfections can be worked around; determine if there's enough salvageable fabric. Best to refrain from purchasing unless fabric will serve its purpose, for example, as a specimen for study groups or for fabric swaps.

Buying, Pricing, and Thread Count

The Importance of Thread Count

For the fabric collector, thread count is mostly associated with percale and muslin because of the value placed on thread counts for bed sheets, dress percales, and dress muslins.

Thread count and yarn count are different. Thread count, also called cloth count, is the number of warp and filling yarns in a square inch of fabric; yarn count measures the degree of fineness of the yarn. Thread count is given either as a single number representing the total of warp and filling yarns to the inch or as separate numbers for total each of warp and filling threads — in most cases, there will always be more warp yarns as they are first to be set up on the loom and serve as supports as columns are to architecture. For example, a sheet could be advertised as a 140-thread count (meaning 74 warp yarns, 66 filling yarns), or as 74 x 66.

The closer in count of warp and filling yarns, the more balanced fabric will be but that does not mean it is a better fabric. Some weaves, like broadcloth, require more warp yarns as part of its construction design. Sometimes the filling or warp can be of poor yarn quality. One has to consider both yarn quality and thread count in determining the suitability of fabrics.

To test a fabric's strength, hold fabric with both hands and press down and apart, with thumbs close together and parallel. Weak yarns will split; low count will cause threads to slide or spread apart. A good rule to remember is a high-count fabric with a poor balance will give better wear than a low-count fabric with a good balance.

Muslin and Percale	Thread Count Comparison Count Per Square Inch	Grade and Quality
Muslin, back-filled	less than 112 threads	Loosely woven; heavy sizing lost after wash; turns sleazy
Muslin, lightweight	not less than 112 threads	Wears well, but has limited service
Muslin, medium weight	not less than 128 threads	Strong, satisfactory wear
Muslin, heavyweight	not less than 140 threads	Sturdy, longest wearing muslin
Percale, dress fabric	160 threads	Lightweight, durable, smooth, usually listed as 80 sq.
Percale, carded	not less than 180 threads	Lightweight, made from all-carded yarns
Percale, combed	not less than 180 threads	Lightweight, smooth, durable, made from all-combed yarns
Percale, finest	not less than 200 threads	Most luxurious; made of finest all-combed or pima yarns

Fabric Identification by Fiber, Weave, and Appearance

Identification by Fiber and Burn Test

Fibers are obtained from many sources: animal, vegetable, plant, and test tube. Natural fibers are those from wool, cotton, flax, hemp, jute, and ramie and are of limited length. Filaments are of continuous lengths. Silk is a secreted filament from the silkworm, and manufactured fibers are extruded filaments forced through spinnerets. Shown here are the basic fibers in each classification which fall within our timetable. For a complete range of fibers, textile science or technology books are recommended.

There are several ways for the lay person to determine a fabric's fiber, although for blends and percentages, a professional laboratory analysis is needed. However, two simple analyses can be obtained with a microscope and burn test. The burn test can be conducted using about five or six yarns bundled together or a 1" to 2" swatch of fabric which can often give better results. Light match to fabric while holding over an ashtray or dish and let it drop into container to burn. Another method is to use tweezers to hold yarn or fabric as it burns. As a precaution, have baking soda or water handy in case flare-up should get out of control. If you are using a microscope, an inexpensive one with an 150 magnification is recommended (15x eyepiece x 10x objective).

Cotton Plant, Cellulose

Burn Test: ignites rapidly; burns quickly with yellow flame; continues to burn when removed from flame with afterglow; light feathery, grayish–black ashes; burning paper odor. Cotton/poly blend will produce an oil well (a tall, brightly burning flame surrounded by black smoke) and an unpleasant odor. Residue is black goo.

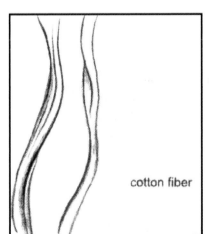

cotton fiber

Artist's view of cotton fiber as it appears under the microscope. Jessica McClure, artist.

You can grow your own cotton plant with this seed packet. Courtesy National Cotton Council of America.

Silkworm, Protein

Burn test: pure dye silk smolders, burns with difficulty, melts slowly, sputters, ceases flaming when removed from flame; round, crisp, shiny black beads easily crushed. Odor same as wool but not as strong. Weighted silk burns with glow, then chars.

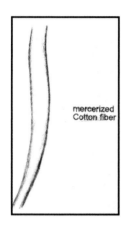
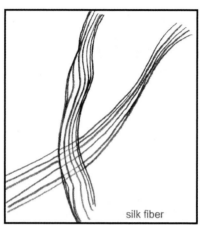

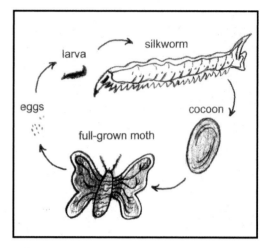

Artist's view of silk and raw silk filaments as they appear under the microscope. Jessica McClure, artist.

Silkworm cycle drawn by Isaac Murcar, nine, who raised silkworms at age five.

Wool, Sheep, Protein

Burn test: smolders as nears flame; small, slow flickering flame; sizzles and curls, ceases flaming when removed; crisp, dark ash, irregular shape, crushes easily; burning hair or feathers odor. Wool will also dissolve in chlorine bleach.

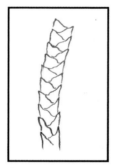

Artist view of wool fiber as it looks under the microscope. Jessica McClure, artist.

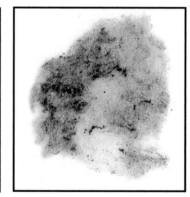

Long-wooled Romney sire produces coarse wool used for tweeds, overcoating, carpets and other industrial fabrics. Courtesy American Sheep Industry Association Inc. Raw wool. The late Pauline Bulawa collection.

Linen, Flax

Burn test: ignites easily and scorches; burns slower than cotton especially with heavier yarns, continues to burn when removed; feather, grey ash; burning paper odor. Similar to cotton. Squeeze test: pull yarn through two tightly compressed fingertips; linen will emerge stiff and straight; cotton, limp.

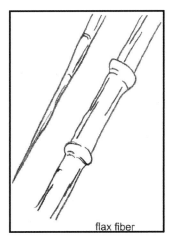

Artist's view of linen fiber as it appears under the microscope. Jessica McClure, artist.

Flax plant from which linen is derived. Jessica McClure, artist.

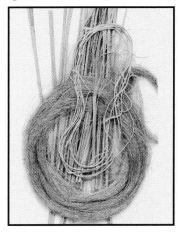

Flax straw from which is produced the fine linen fiber shown here (called line), and a coarser, shorter fiber called tow (not shown). The late Pauline Bulawa collection. Also shown is fine linen thread handspun from homegrown flax in Northeast Pennsylvania, 1910 – 1912, and used to weave cloth for family clothing. Linda Learn family heirloom collection.

Burn Tests for Manufactured Fibers

Rayon

Viscose and cuprammonium rayon, reconstituted cellulose fibers, are the oldest manufactured fiber — ignites and burns quickly, yellow flame similar to cotton. Continues to burn after removed from flame, no afterglow. Light, grey feathery ashes. Burning paper odor.

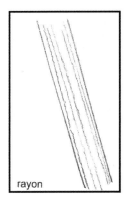

Artist's view of rayon filament as it appears under the microscope. Jessica McClure, artist.

Rayon filament and staple fiber from *Facts about Fabrics*, c. 1950s. Courtesy E.I. Du Pont de Nemours and Company.

Raw fibers of Merinova, one of several brand names for milk protein (azlon) blended with rayon which is similar to Aralac shown in "Fabrics on Parade," rayon Ara-fab dress, page 92. Mary Humphries collection.

Acetate

Acetate, modified rayon — fuses away from flame, burns black. Flames quickly, sputters, melts, drips like burning tar as fabric puckers. Continues to burn and melt when removed from flame. Vinegar odor. Brittle, hard, irregular black ash, difficult to crush. Acetate will also dissolve in acetone (nail polish remover).

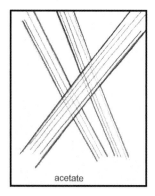

Artist's view of acetate filament as it appears under the microscope. Jessica McClure, artist.

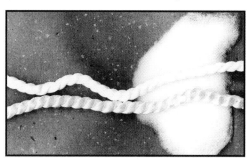

Acetate staple textile fiber with dull and bright acetate yarns. The late Pauline Bulawa collection.

Nylon

Nylon, polyamide, the first synthetic fiber — fuses and shrinks from flame; burns slowly with melting; flame diminishes and tends to die out; odor has celery smell. Hard, round, tough grey bead.

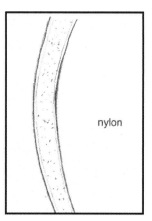

Artist's view of nylon filament as it appears under the microscope. Jessica McClure, artist.

Polyester

Polyester (Dacron, Kodel and Fortrel for example) — fuses and shrinks away from flame; leaves a hard, round bead which can't be crushed; pungent odor.

Artist's view of poly filament as it appears under the microscope. Jessica McClure, artist.

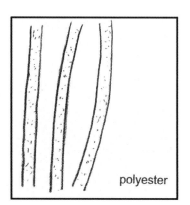

Fabric Identification by Weave Structure

It is remarkable that with the hundreds of different textures and appearances fabrics offer, there are only three foundation or basic weaves in clothmaking — plain or tabby, twill and satin. All others are variations of these weaves, alone or in combination. In fact, there has not been any new weave created since 1747 when a book of weaves was published in Berlin, Germany. Leno (doup), dobby, jacquard, box, lappet, and swivel weaves which require special loom mechanisms or attachments are often added to this list as they are weaves in their own right.

A weave is described as a system of interlacing threads of warp and filling according to a defined procedure to produce a textile. A binding system is the way ends (warp yarns) and picks (filling yarns) are bound to produce the weaves mentioned above. To remember direction of yarns, warp runs north/south and pick (or filling yarn) runs east/west. It is the interlacing of these two yarns on the loom which produces a weave and gives fabric its structure and texture.

An indispensable aid for revealing a weave is a special magnifier called a linen tester or thread or pick counter. When tester is laid on fabric, the weave structure immediately pops up and for those counting threads, the enlarged viewing is ideal. Testers are at their optimum in 9x, 9x double lens, and 10x; however 8x will give satisfactory results. Shown here are the three foundation weaves plus leno, jacquard, and dobby weaves. Lappet and swivel weaves are shown in the following look-alikes section under dotted Swiss.

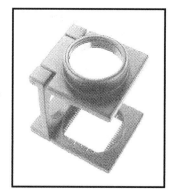

Linen tester, folds flat for storage.
Image courtesy Indigo® Instruments.

Twill Weave — Diagnol Lines
Filling interlaces with two to four warp yarns. Each line of filling moves one step right to form diagonal.

twill weave

Twill weave. Jessica McClure, artist.

Plain or Tabby Weave
Each filling yarn goes alternately over and under each warp across width.

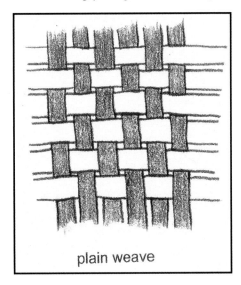

Plain weave. Jessica McClure, artist.

Satin Weave
Similar to twill but weave is not visible. Warp yarns are arranged to conceal filling or vice versa, thus allowing maximum reflection of light on surface which gives most lustrous and smoothest look possible.

Satin weave, warp face. Jessica McClure, artist.

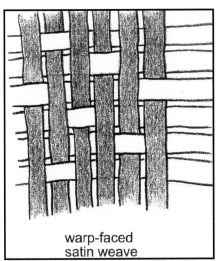

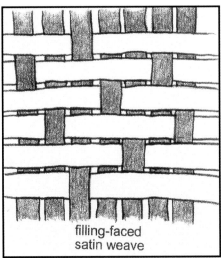

Satin weave, filling face. Jessica McClure, artist.

Leno or Doup Weave

Warp yarns diagonally cross other warp yarns between filling yarns. Allows widely spaced yarns to be firmly held in place. An onion sack is a good example of this weave. Another term, gauze weave which was a slight variation of the leno weave, was discontinued about 30 years ago to simplify and eliminate confusion about the name of this weave.

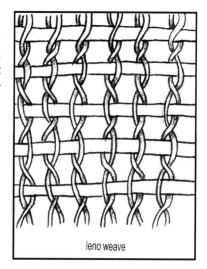

Leno weave. Jessica McClure, artist.

Jacquard Weave

Sophisticated loom for producing unlimited range of large intricate designs, swirls and curves.

Rayon brocade, example of jacquard weave.

Dobby Weave

Cam mechanism or loom for creating small geometric patterned weaves which cannot be produced by jacquard loom.

Fancy barkcloth, example of dobby weave.

Fabric Identification by Appearance: The Look-alikes

There are some fabrics which resemble each other thus causing confusion and their names to be interchanged — grenadine and marquisette, plissé and seersucker, and starchless lawn (lawn organdy) and organdy are common examples. Here are some guidelines to help distinguish which fabric is which, plus a dotted Swiss primer.

Grenadine and Marquisette – Leno Weave

Grenadine, which resembles organza, is a very fine mesh version of marquisette. When mesh measures about ¹⁄₁₆" it becomes marquisette. While seldom mentioned by their rightful names today, both fabrics exist primarily as curtain sheers. Grenadine can be found in fancy shadow-stripe organzas or other sheers of allover leno weave. Marquisette is used for veiling and for overskirts for dress and formal wear. A linen tester is required to detect both leno weave and mesh fineness. For fabric description, see "Fabrics on Parade," page 46, for Grenandine; page 60 for Marquisette.

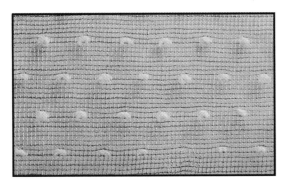

Marquisette, example of a leno weave.

Plissé and Seersucker

Plain weave cotton crepes. In its simplest definition, plissé rippling or blistering is created chemically; seersucker rippling is created during weaving by slacking tension on some warps or groups of warp yarns. A magnifying glass will help you to differentiate. Plissé — where blisters are puffy on right side there will be indentations on wrong side. Sticking a straight pin through a blister pinpoints its hollowness on reverse side. Seersucker — wrong side reveals rippled striping made by slackened threads. You can actually see and feel these threads which are formed by holding alternate groups of warps yarns slack in the loom during weaving. This type of woven pattern is called shape retentive because pattern is made permanent by weaving. Another way to distinguish these two fabrics is to pull away about five rows of filling yarn. Plissé will show no extra warp yarns; seersucker will reveal extra warps in each striping or rippling area.

Comparison of enlarged views of frayed ends of plissé and seersucker reveal no extra warp yarns in plissé. Upper part of photo is reverse side showing clearer indentations made by chemical creping (blistering, rippling). Note the extra warp yarns in rippled sections of seersucker created during weaving process and the use of dyed yarns to create pattern as opposed to the printed pattern on plissé.

Starchless Lawn, Lawn Organdy, Swiss Muslin and Organdy

Starchless lawns, including Swiss muslin, have a crisp finish and are often mistaken for organdy and vice versa. There is a way to tell the difference.

Starchless lawn – Semi-or permanent soft crisp to crisp finish, sometimes called an organdy finish, which is given to lawn, fine muslin, and mull and sometimes nainsook. These lawns are also called lawn organdy or poorman's Swiss muslin which can be an exceptionally superior India muslin or lawn. See page 140 – 142 for the many brand names for starchless finishes. As finish is not stiff, when fabric is grasped in hand and manually gathered, gathers will fall in graceful, fine folds and hold their drape.

Organdy – Stiff, usually permanent finish given to lawn which is the favored fabric for organdy but is made also of voile and fine muslin and other quality semi-sheers. Best quality organdies are given a Heberlein finish which produces a surface as smooth and silky as an ice-skating surface. When gathered by hand or machine, gathers will be bulky and bunch unevenly rather than fall into graceful, evenly distributed folds like starchless lawn.

Using swatches of the same size, the soft crispness of starchless lawn or lawn organdy enables fabric to produce finer gathers in the same amount of space while organdy's stiffness produces bulky, irregular gathering.

Dotted Swiss

There are two types of dotted Swiss: woven and printed which includes flocking.

Woven — Made with swivel or lappet or box looms. Lawn, voile, and organdy and fine muslin are the preferred dress fabrics; muslin, fine gauze, and scrim for curtains.

Swivel and clip spot — Swivel wraps around warp yarns like a whip stitch with a fastening at each end per each motif. For clipspot, floats between each dots or figures are woven in fabric using extra filling or filling yarns which produce a shaggy surface on one side from filling ends which have been cut. Real Swiss swivel dot has only two clipped ends and is the rarest, most expensive but best wearing. Today it is mostly made on the jacquard loom. A clip spot has two ends clipped of each filling forming the dot. Most woven dotted Swiss is clip spot. Clipspot is also called clip dot, spot dot, and American dotted Swiss.

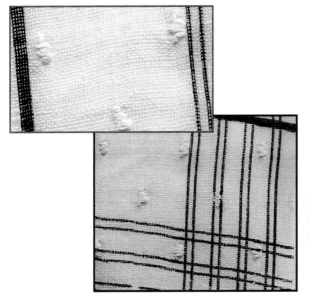

Examples of clipspot with enlarged view of its swivel weave on 1940s – 1950s fine, crisp lawn, and a fancy swivel weave motif on 1918 – 1920 fine muslin.

Lappet — Lappet forms outline stitches as it climbs filling yarns and fastens at end of each motif with knot. Dots or figures woven in or embroidered on fabric using extra warp yarns. Dots are clipped; yarn floats on other patterns. When dots are cut on the surface, they are called eyelash. Lappet is rarely seen and not made in the U.S.

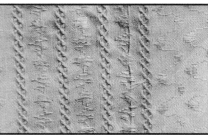

Lappet weave motifs on a 1930s fine semi-sheer lawn with enlarged view of lappet weave structure.

Box loom — Creates embroidered design for fabrics made with two or more colors in the filling

Box loom — 1950s French heavy silk satin with embroidered multi-color design showing right and wrong sides.

Printed — Process is a chemical application which applies a raised or flat design or dots either as color only or by flocking. It was known as appliqué prior to early 1900s, composition dot or paste dot to around 1928, then flocking by which dots of glue are printed on the ground and short fibers applied to them, and the current method which is the printed or duco dot for printing or painted on the ground.

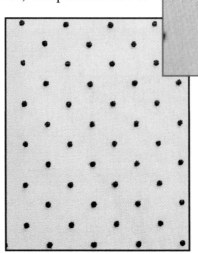

1940s Velveray flocked dot on organdy with enlarged view.

Dating Dotted Swiss — These are guidelines given in the broadest sense only for estimating dates of dotted Swiss:

Before 1930s — Woven dots were larger, at least ¼" to ½", and spaced farther apart. See swivel clip spot photo, page 129. 1930s — measles effect with smaller dots spaced closer together. See 1930s dotted Swiss photo, page 130.

1940s — A return to slightly larger dots and wider spacing. Flocked and pair dotting also popular. See 1940s flocked dot photo, page 130.

1950s — Return to 1930s style and pair dotting. Flocking is ever seasonal, appearing as a fashion trend in any given year.

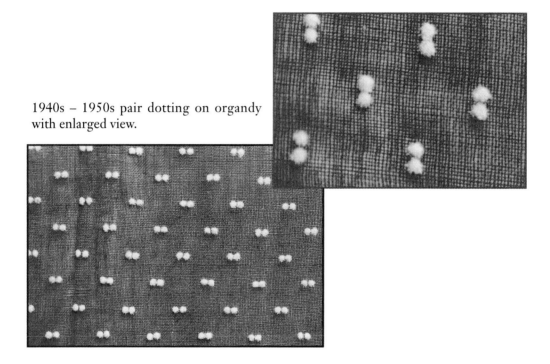

1940s – 1950s pair dotting on organdy with enlarged view.

1950s plasticized flock dots on voile.

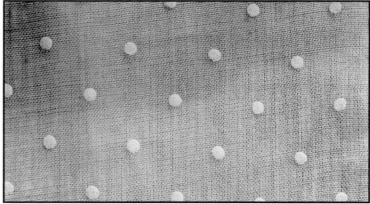

Fabric Identification by Width, Brand Names, Finishes, and Mills

As you hold a piece of fabric in your hand, the desire to know more about it beyond its fiber is compelling. What is its name? What is this texture? Who manufactured it? What was it used for and when?

Few are fortunate to acquire old unwashed fabric with a provenance that tells something of its past. A brand name or other markings imprinted in the selvage, for instance, or a manufacturer's label still intact or a family pass-me-on neatly labeled with name or date, sometimes a sales slip or a notation for its use.

Without such aids, name and dating identifications often end up an educated guess, particularly for less commonly recognized fabrics, those which look alike and those which have been washed. And add to that the retro and repro prints which are so popular for quilting today and which can be so misleading to the lay person.

Yet there are certain indicators which can help to narrow the identification process through cursory examination — fabric width, weave and texture, color, pattern or design, even an overall appearance which has an acquired patina. Those persons with dye expertise, a complex scientific field not covered here, can take identification one step further.

All capitalized brand names in this chapter automatically include trademark and registration symbols.

Common Widths, 1880s — 1959

Width is usually the first place of inspection for collectors, particularly for cottons. The unofficial but universally understood 36" width which represents most dressmaking cottons sets a closing date of sorts.

Generally, 24" width indicates the average cotton standard prior to 1900 although in 1871 brown (unbleached or grey goods) and bleached cottons were being manufactured in 33", 36", 40", 45", and 48" widths; that was increased to 27" to 32" through the 1930s; and 36", 40", and 42" through the 1960s. It should be noted that Liberty of London still produces 36" width lawn, and some Japanese firms still produce narrow silk cloth, but these are the exceptions.

For the most part, 42" to 44" widths in cotton became the dominant and then prevailing width by the early 1960s – early 1970s. The trend today is towards wider widths; many of the fine Swiss imports such as voile, lawn, batiste, and dotted Swiss are now available 60" wide and loommakers hint at even wider widths to come.

However, these are only indicators and not gospel. We tend to think of wider widths as modern innovations but this is far from fact. Collectors should become familiar with the variety of widths available in any given time period. Catalogs and textile glossaries are invaluable references for providing this information.

The following chart tracks the prevailing widths of staple and common cloths from late 1880s to 1959. These were found in Sears, Montgomery Ward, and other catalogs, old textile glossaries, magazines, and advertisements. Many catalogs prior to WWI did not always specify width for every fabric, being more concerned with giving correct total yardage for dresses and gowns which automatically took into consideration fabric widths. Therefore the width ranges given here do not preclude the availability of widths outside of these ranges.

Chart of Prevailing Common Fabric Widths 1880-1959. Excludes upholstery, utility, and narrow fabrics.

Cotton and Linen	1880 – 1900	1900 – 1915	1916 – 1930	1931 – 1939	1940 – 1949	1950 – 1959
batiste – all types	32 – 40"	32 – 42"	28 – 45"	35 – 45"	36 – 39"	36 – 39"
broadcloth & shirtings	22 – 33"	22 – 33"	24 – 36"	34 – 36"	33 – 36"	36 – 44"
calico, indigo & dress muslin	21 – 38"	21 – 34"	25 – 36"	27 – 36"	33 – 36"	36"
cambric	25 – 36"	25 – 36"	25 – 45"	36"	36"	36"
challis	26 – 31"	26 – 31"	23 – 36"	27 – 54"	36"	36"
chambray	22 – 33"	22 – 33"	27 – 36"	25 – 36"	32 – 36"	36"
chintz, glazed	not found by this name		25 – 36"	25 – 50"	28 – 48"	36 – 48"
corduroy	27 – 28"	27 – 28"	27 – 36"	36 – 40"	35 – 36"	36 – 37; 54"
dimity - all types	26 – 30"	26 – 36"	27 – 39"	32 – 36"	35 – 36"	36"
fancies, novelties	25 – 30"	25 – 28"	27 – 39"	27 – 36"	36"	36 – 40"
fine, plain, colorfast, & drip dry, wash 'n' wear brand names	27 – 32"	27 – 32"	27 – 36"	36 – 40"	36 – 39"	36 – 45"
flannel - all types	25 – 36"	25 – 36"	26 – 36"	26 – 36"	27 – 38"	36"
gingham	25 – 32"	25 – 32"	26 – 40"	26 – 36"	34 – 44"	36 – 44"
home décor – crash, cretonne, bark, chintz	25 – 36"	25 – 36"	34 – 50"	34 – 36"	36 – 48"	36 – 60"
Indian Head	33 – 63"	33 – 63"	33 – 63"	33 – 63"	33 – 53"	36 – 53"
lawn - all types	20 – 41"	24 – 48"	27 – 45"	27 – 45"	36 – 40"	36 – 40"
linen, dress	30"	31 – 36"	36 – 45"	36"	36"	36 – 54"
longcloth	32"	32"	36 – 45"	36 – 45"	36"	off market
mull	29 – 32"	29 – 32"	29 – 45"	36 – 45"	off market	off market
nainsook - all types	25 – 48"	25 – 36"	36 – 45"	36 – 45"	36"	36"
organdy	30 – 32"	30 – 68"	32 – 72"	36 – 45"	36 – 45"	36 – 44"
percale	36"	36"	36"	36"	36"	36"
piqué	25"	25 – 32"	27 – 36"	27 – 37"	34 – 36"	36"
plissé, crepes	28"	28"	29 – 36"	29 – 36"	29 – 36"	29 – 36
poplin	no listing	no listing	27 – 39"	27 – 36"	33 – 36"	36 – 40"

Cotton and Linen	1880 – 1900	1900 – 1915	1916 – 1930	1931 – 1939	1940 – 1949	1950 – 1959
sateen	25 – 32"	25 – 39"	25 – 37"	25 – 39; 50"	30 – 39; 50"	30 – 40; 50"
seersucker	27"	27"	27 – 32"	29 – 36"	36"	36 – 40"
Swiss, dotted types	25"	25"	27 – 45"	28 – 36"	36 – 39"	36 – 40"
velveteen	18 – 24"	18 – 24"	24 – 29"	36 – 39"	36 – 39"	36 – 39"
voile	25 – 30"	25 – 30"	33 – 45"	36 – 40"	36 – 40"	36 – 40"

Silk	1880 – 1900	1900 – 1915	1916 – 1930	1931 – 1939	1940 – 1949	1950 – 1959
bengaline	18 – 22"	18 – 22"	22 – 40"	40"	40"	40"
crepes	18 – 40"	18 – 40"	35 – 54"	34 – 40"	39 – 40"	40 – 45"
faille	19"	19"	36 – 40"	36 – 40"	36 – 40"	39 – 40"
moiré	18 – 22"	18 – 22"	22 – 40"	27 – 40"	39 – 40"	40 – 45"
novelties, fancies	18 – 27"	18 – 27"	18 – 36"	38 – 39"	38 – 45"	38 – 45"
satin	19 – 36"	19 – 36"	19 – 40"	37 – 52"	39 – 42"	39 – 42"
taffeta	18 – 19"	19 – 36"	35 – 36"	36 – 40"	39 – 42"	39 – 42"
velvet	18 – 25"	18 – 24"	24 – 29"	36 – 39"	36 – 39"	36 – 39"
flats & all others	18 – 43"	18 – 45"	27 – 46"	32 – 54"	38 – 45"	40 – 45"

Wool	1880 – 1900	1900 – 1915	1916 – 1930	1931 – 1939	1940 – 1949	1950 – 1959
broadcloth	50 – 54"	50 – 54"	50 – 54"	50 – 54"	54"	54"
flannel & gabardine	23 – 45"	27 – 50"	26 – 54"	40 – 54"	44 – 54"	44 – 54"
serge	24 – 36"	36 – 54"	35 – 60"	44 – 60"	44 – 60"	50 – 60"
suitings, fancies & blends	27 – 40"	33 – 46"	36 – 60"	44 – 60"	44 – 60"	50 – 60"
all other wools	18 – 54"	18 – 54"	24 – 54"	44 – 54"	44 – 54"	44 – 60"

Rayon & Acetate	1880 – 1900	1900 – 1915	1916 – 1930	1931 – 1939	1940 – 1949	1950 – 1959
blends, suitings	NA	NA	35 – 40"	35 – 54"	38 – 60"	38 – 60"
velvet & velveteen			see cotton and silk			
flats, crepes & all others	NA	NA	35 – 39"	35 – 39"	38 – 42"	39 – 48"

Synthetics	1880 – 1900	1900 – 1915	1916 – 1930	1931 – 1939	1940 – 1949	1950 – 1959
nylon & blends	NA	NA	NA	NA	NA	36 – 45"
Dacron, Arnel	NA	NA	NA	NA	NA	36 – 45"

Common Brand Names of Fabrics and Finishes

It is always a help in the identification process when you acquire old fabric that has a name printed in the selvage, stamped on the cloth, or on an attached manufacturer's label. Many manufacturers were proud of their fabrics and lavishly extolled in ads to the consumer to look for their name or brand name which was printed in the selvage every yard or every three yards, etc. Selvage markings carrying both manufacturer and brand name are especially welcome news. It is not unusual to find persons who collect only selvage markings, logos, and labels. Listed here are brand names which are traceable to their source which could be a mill, manufacturer or distributor. Rayon and nylon are listed separately. Also see mill information on pages 143 – 154 for cross reference.

ABC Fabrics – Arthur Beir & Co.; fine zephyrs, silk and cotton prints, Buty satinette, batiste, dimity, 80 sq. fast-color percales.

Alltyme and Alltyme Crepe – Edwin E. Berliner & Co.; cotton, wool, silk, rayon, and flax fibers.

Argentine Cloth Bunting – Jenkins, Kreer & Co.; glazed tarlatan.

Baronette – Duplan Silk Corp.; a sports fabric of cotton-backed silk satin.

Belle Island Muslin – Made for J.C. Penney; sheeting muslin.

Blue-Bonnets – Lesher-Whitman & Co.; finest dress fabrics.

Bontax – H. B. Clafins; fine wash fabrics, ratinés and crepes, name in selvage.

Brandenburg Prints – Simpson Co.; prints, satines, fine percales.

Bulldog – J.L. Stifel & Sons; twilled shirting.

Charmeen – Forstmann Inc. (Victor Forstmann); fine worsted steep twill.

Cheveret – Ingram Interlining Co.; interlinings.

Cinderella – Johnson-Cowles-Emmerich; satin two tones.

Cloqué – Everfast Fabric; novelty birdseye piqué.

Cloth of Gold, Bluebird-Cloth of Gold – According to 1984 and 1990 *Ladies Circle Patchwork Quilts* magazine, CoG was the name of a converter of piece goods specializing in a line of fine cottons — lawn, batiste, nainsook, dimity, muslin, and using the name of an old-time favorite fabric which was woven and dyed in different southern mills and distributed by various companies and which became synonymous with quality cotton piece goods. During the 1920s, *Farmers Wife* quilting booklets recommended and sold pure white Cloth of Gold for quilt backing, guaranteed not to yellow.

Clydella – Wm. Hollins & Co. Ltd., UK; patented 19% wool and 81% cotton mixture.

Cordino – Made for J. C. Penney; fine cotton wale similar to Bedford cord.

Crepe Meteor – Cheney Bros.; silk satin.

Daisy Bell – Made for Marshall Field's & Co.; fast-color muslin.

Daisy Cloth – Amoskeag Mfg. Co.; flannel, napped cloth.

Devonshire Cloth – Renfrew Mfg. Co.; Scotty dog logo name on selvage.

Diana – Puritan Mills; sunfast, washfast cotton.

Dolly Madison – American Printing Co.; muslin made for Sears.

Durene – Durene Assn. of America; fine combed, mercerized cotton.

Duretta – Pacific Mills (Springs Industries); twilled fabric, lustre finish.

Eddystone – Simpson Eddystone Mfg. Co.; hazel brown fast print calicoes.

Elberon – Imitation silk velvet; name stamped on selvage.

Everfast Fabrics – N. Erlanger, Blumgart & Co.; washfast, sunfast cotton.

Finesse – Nashua Mfg. Co.; carried Indian Head name, a fine plain, possibly broadcloth.

Fluff-O-Down – Elder & Johnston; flannels of Australian wool and Sea Island cotton.

Fibre Chamois – American Fibre Chamois Co.; waterproofed interlining.

Flaxon – Ponemah Mills and Federated Textiles; fine line of luster-finish cottons; name printed on every yard. Dates back to at least 1890s as a generic name for a popular line of shirtwaist and summer dress fabrics.

Fruit of the Loom – B.B. & R. Knight (Burlington Industries/ITG); fine cottons.

Geron – Forstmann Div., J.P. Stevens (Victor Forstmann); a type of wool-pile bolivia.

Gilberta – H. B. Clafins, Inc.; piece goods, lining, partly or wholly of cotton, wool and silk.

Gilbrae Fabric – Ely & Walker (more likely the selling agent or distributor); ginghams and fine cottons.

Hair Cloth – American Hair Cloth Co.; hair cloth crinoline interlining, pure hair filling, resilient, will not break, stretch or crush.

Harris Tweed – Harris Tweed Assn. Cloth made of pure virgin wool that is produced, spun and handwoven in Scotland by islanders. Wool is then returned to mills where it is washed, marked and sent to buyers under the Harris Tweed signature.

Heatherbloom – Fred Butterfield & Co. Inc.; cotton taffeta for linings.

Hopewell – Pontiac Bleachery; soft-finished goods.

Indian Head – Jackson Mills (1831), Nashua Mfg. Co. (1916); 1941 – 1945 off market due to WWII; Textron (1948); Indian Head Mills Inc. 1953 – 1975; discontinued 1961. First known as Jackson sheeting, then named Indian Head in 1831; a superior linen-textured muslin; name also given to percale and broadcloth lines.

Ironclad – Moneyworth; galatea.

Jerray – Waycroft Mills; jersey cloth of wool and rayon blend.

Kalburnie – Lancaster Mills; fine ginghams.

Khaki Kool – H. R. Mallinson & Co. Inc.; sports silk similar to Baronette, see listing.

Kiddie Cloth – H. B. Clafins, Inc.; a line of sturdy ginghams.

Kitten's Ear Crepe – Haas Bros.; Silk Fabric Corp.; silk.

Landsdowne – Wm. F. Read; for fine silk/wool dress fabrics; perforated name every 3 yards.

Linnette – Harlomoor Co.; chased-finished duck.

Lorganza, l'Organza – Bianchini Ferier; patented silk organza in early 1950s, wirier than traditional organza and silk organdy; name has become a generic and now called organza, and is the most prevalent type on the market.

Lotus Cloth – Lowell Weaving; fine dress goods, brilliancy and luster of silk, mercerized yarns.

Lustercale – Wamsutta Mills (Springs Industries); highly mercerized cotton used mostly for sheeting.

Marvella – Forstmann Div., J.P. Stevens (Victor Forstmann); a type of wool-pile bolivia.

Merrimack Duckling Fleece – Merrimack Mfg. Co.; name stamped in selvage, flannel for kimonos, bathrobes.

Milateen – Forstmann Inc. (Victor Forstmann); fine worsted dress fabric similar to but heavier than Charmeen, see listing.

Miss Stifel Indigo Cloth – J.L. Stifel & Sons; type of Bulldog twill.

Moygashel Linen – Moygashel, Ltd., 1953 to sold Stevenson & Sons Ltd., 1969 now a subsidiary of Courtaulds, Ltd. Excellent quality linen, named after old Gaelic castle of the same name in Dungannon, Ireland as flax grows near this castle. Linen-making at Moygashel dates back 1,500 years. Still in business but only in RTW.

Mulhouse Percales – Mulhouse Mills; featured in Sears & Roebuck 1902 catalog.

Nubia – Fast black cotton dress linings for waists and skirts; percalines, satines, silesias; logo stamped on every yard.

Pamico – Pacific Mills (Springs Industries); sunfast, washfast cotton.

Peter Pan Fabrics and Tinkerbelle Fabrics – Henry Glass (more likely a distributor); color washfast, soft, warm finish in plains, ginghams, woven checks; names with fast color printed in selvages. Peter Pan now owned by Marcus Bros.

Picolay – Bates Fabric Co.; sunfast, washfast cottons and percales.

Polo Cloth – Worumbo Mfg. Co., J.P. Stevens; camel's wool coating.

Polly Prim – Henry Glass & Co. (more likely a distributor); a line of fine percales and other fine cottons.

Powder Puff Muslin – Dumari Textile Co.; type of permanent starchless finish dress muslin, guaranteed fast colors.

Pres de Soie – Gilbert Mfg. Co.; drop skirts and petticoats, fast black and colors, soft finish, name in selvage.

Pride of the West – American Bleached Goods; fine, bleached muslin.

Pussy Willow – H.R. Mallinson & Co. Inc.; silk cloth.

Quadriga Cloth – Ely & Walker; needleized fine cotton prints and solids, name stamped on selvage. See E & W in mills section, page 146.

Quaker Lad – Havens & Geddes; longcloth and other cottons.

Radium Silks – Gilbert Mfg. Co.; superior textures, won't split, stretch, or tear.

Ramona Cloth – Made for J. C. Penney; heavy cotton with linen-like finish.

Renfrew Fabrics – Renfrew Mfg.; ginghams, colored wash fabrics, fast colors.

Repent and Sell – Fred Butterfield & Co. Inc.; cotton, wool, silk piece goods. This is a favorite name among collectors to acquire.

Ripplette – Androscoggin Mills, Bates Fabric. Co.; name marked on every selvage; cotton plissé, solids, stripes, bedspreads.

Roshanara – H.R. Mallinson Co.; heavy crepe rib texture in silk/wool, rayon/wool, or rayon/cotton.

Romper Cloth – Amoskeag Mfg. Co.; sturdy line of ginghams.

Seco – Silk mull, usually cotton warp, spun silk filling.

Serpentine Crepe – Pacific Mills (Springs Industries); Dolly Varden, Dresden and Cubist designs, name printed on every selvage.

Sherette – Sherman and Sons; fine line of cottons similar to Flaxon.

Silcot – Made for Marshall Field & Co. Inc.; silk and cotton blend.

Soisette – Ponemah Mills; name dates back to at least 1890s when it was copyrighted by Clarence Whitrand & Co.; fine cotton pongee prints and solids which resembled silk; name printed on every yard; name changed to Soisette-Tubfast in 1927.

Sponge Crepon – Sponge Cloth Mfg. Co.; waterproofed interlining and stiffening, perforated for summer wear, elastic, unbreakable, never loses shape, fast black colors, name in red selvage.

Sunfast Fabrics – Orinoka Mills, Joseph Bancroft & Sons; quality color-fast cottons.

SuPima – SuPima Association of America; fine quality cottons made from pima yarn only; use of name controlled and licensed by the Association.

Tarpoon – Galey & Lord Div., Burlington Industries, Inc.; water repellant sportsweight gingham.

Tommy Tucker – Milldale Textiles; "Tommy Tucker Guarantee Fast-Color" stamped in every selvage.

Triam cottons – Pacific Mills (Springs Industries); quality line of cottons.

Tubrite – Cohn-Hall-Marx NYC; washfast fabrics.

Velutina – waterproofed imitation silk velvet; name stamped in selvage.

Viyella – Wm. Hollins & Co. Ltd., sold to Birmingham Group; patented at 55% merino wool and 45% fine English cotton blend flannel. Currently available as RTW only.

Popular Brand Name Finishes

Often a fabric was or is more famous or desirable for its appearance and wearable features. Here are some of the more prevalent names which were popular with consumers. In some instances, due to varying availability, cited in reference sources, date ranges are given for their appearance on the market.

Anti-Crease – Tootal Broadhurst Lee Co., 1936; wrinkle, crease control.

Apponize – W.E. McKay & Co., 1942 – 1947; starchless finish.

Ban-dri – Joseph Bancroft & Sons, 1936 – 1942; water, spot & stain proof.

Basco – Joseph Bancroft & Sons, 1922 – 1925; permanent linenized finish.

Belfast – Deering Millikin Research Corp., 1942 – 1947; self-ironing finish for cotton.

Bellman – Brook Bleachery, 1936 – 1942; permanent starchless finish.

Cravenette, Cravennette Long Life, Cravenette Plus, Cravenette 330 – U.S. Cravenetting Co., 1916; water and stain proof.

Cyana – American Cyanamid Co., 1947 – 1953; wrinkle free and stain control for cotton.

Disciplined – Bates Mfg. Co, 1947 – 1953; wrinkle free and stain control on cotton.

Everglaze – Cyrus Clark, Joseph Bancroft & Sons, 1936 – 1942; durable starchless and washable glaze finish.

Evershrunk – Everfast Fabrics, 1942 – 1947; shrinkage control.

Fibredown – Arnold Fabrics, 1936 – 1942; flock dot application process.

Fibreglas – Owens Corning Co., 1936; glass fiber enhancement.

Glosheen – Waverly Fabrics, 1936 – 1942; super glazing finish for sateen.

Heberlein – Heberlein Patent Corp., 1942 – 1947; Swiss finish for permanent crispness.

Koroseal – B. F. Goodrich Co.; 1936 – 1942; water repellency and stain guard for all fibers but acetate.

Lanaset – American Cyanamid Co., 1942 – 1947; shrinkage control.

Martinized – Martin Fabrics Co., 1936 – 1942; wrinkle and crease control.

Neva-Wet – Neva-Wet Corp. of America, 1936 – 1942; waterproofing.

Pacific Stabilized Fabric – Worsted Div., Pacific Mills, 1947 – 1953; anti-wrinkle and shrink control for wool.

Pluette – The Pluette Co., Shaen Mfg., 1890s; waterproof treatment for serge, storm serge, name stamped every six yards.

Rainfoe – Schwarzwalder Co., 1947 – 1952; durable water repellent finish.

Rigby Process – Rigby Waterproof and Finishing, 1890s; treatment for waterproofing linings.

Sabel – Kendall Mills, 1942 – 1947; starchless finish.

Sanforize, Sanforize-Shrunk, Sanforlan – Sanforized Div., Cluett Peabody & Co., 1930; process to have shrinkage less than 1% for cotton and linen; renamed Sanforized by 1942.

Saylerize – Sayler Finishing Plants, 1942 – 1947; permanent starchless finish.

Sheercroft – Joseph Bancroft & Sons, 1936 – 1942; permanent starchless finish.

Sheerset – American Cyananid Co., 1942 – 1947; permanent starchless finish.

Stazenu – Joseph Bancroft & Sons 1947 – 1953; wrinkle and crease control.

Stayz-rite – Joseph Bancroft & Sons, 1936 – 1942; permanent starchless finish.

Superset – American Cyanamid Co., 1947 – 1953; wrinkle and crease control.

Tebilizing – Tootal Broadhurst Lee Co., 1936 – 1942; wrinkle and crease control.

Tubize – Tubize Chatillon Corp.,1930s; process for washable nitrocellulose rayon and rayons made by viscose and acetate processes.

Vita-last – U.S. Finishing Co., 1936 – 1942; permanent starchless finish.

Wat-a-Set – Mt. Hope Finishing Co., 1935 – 1942; shrinkage control.

Wrinkleshed – Dan River Mills Inc., 1947 – 1953; wrinkle and crease control.

Zelan – E.I. duPont de Nemours & Co., 1936 – 1942; waterproofing.

Zeset – E.I. duPont de Nemours Co., 1947 – 1953; wrinkle and crease control.

Common Vintage Man-Made Brand Names

Here are some of the more notable first and second-generation synthetics whose technologies forever changed fiber competition and textile production. Man-made is called manufactured today.

1884 – 1910 Nitrocellulose (Chardonnet process) – Viscose and cuprammonium rayon and acetate processes were introduced. In the U.S., viscose was produced in 1911, acetate 1919 and cuprammonium 1927. Called artificial silk, art silk or fibre silk. By U.S. law in 1924, rayon became the legal name for cellulose-based fibers in this country.

1926 Celanese – Tradename for an acetate rayon, Celanese Corporation of America; Lustron, tradename for acetate rayon; Snia-fil process, Italian process for artificial wool using rayon.

1927 Nylon – Polymer 6,6 or 66, generic name for a synthetic polyamide; withheld from market until end of WWII. Registered by E.I. duPont De Nemours Co. in Belgium, Germany, Italy and Spain, with licensees granted to register in other countries, 49 types.

1927 – 1928 Acele – Tradename for acetate rayon, E.I. duPont de Nemours & Co.; Luminette, MiloSheen and TricoSham, three tradenames for Celanese acetate fabrics, Celanese Corporation of America.

1929 – 1935 Bemburg – Rayon made by cuprammonium process, American Bemburg Co.; Seraceta, rayon made by viscose process, off market by 1953, American Viscose Corp. – not to be confused with Saraceta, an acetate from British Celanese in the early 1960s.

1934 Nitrocellulose – process discontinued; deemed toxic.

1936 – 1942 Crown Tested – Tradename for fabrics from Crown viscose rayon yarns, American Viscose Corp.; Tennessee Eastman Acetate, a type of acetate rayon and Koda, a continuous acetate rayon yarn, Tennessee Eastman Corp; Enka, a type of viscose rayon, American Enka Corp.; Chardonize, a type of viscose rayon, Tubize Chatillon Corp.; Petalqueen, Crown-tested all-spun rayon, Petalspun, Crown-tested flat crepe and Spunblend, 50% rayon viscose, 50% rayon, all Montgomery Ward brands.

1938 Fiberglas – Glass filament developed by Owens-Corning Fiberglas Corp. of

1941 – 1942 Aralac, protein from milk blended with rayon to simulate wool; A..merican Research Associates; discontinued 1948.

1943 – 1947 Avisco – Strong rayon staple, American Viscose Corp, Div of FMC; Textron, tradename for many rayon products, Textron, Inc; Teca, acetate rayon staple fibers often used for blending, Tennessee Eastman Co.

1948 Vicara – Zein from corn blended with rayon and/or nylon, Virginia-Carolina Corp; discontinued 1958.

1949 Chromspun – Solution-dyed rayon yarn, Tennessee Eastman Co.

1950 Acrylonitrile – Generic name for a synthetic polymer to obtain acrylic and modacrylic fiber; Orlon, acrylic fiber resembling wool, 11 types, E.I. duPont de Nemours & Co.

1951 Dynel – Modacrylic fiber, Union Carbide Co.; Acrilan, an acrylic fiber, Chemstrand Corp; Dacron (Br. Terylene), a polyester fiber first known as Fiber V, then Amilar, 20 types, E.I. duPont de Nemours & Co.

1954 Triacetate – Generic term for a modified acetate fiber, Celanese Fibers Co.; Arnel a triacetate resembling wool, Celanese Fibers Co.

1958 Verel – Modacrylic fiber, 6 types, Eastman Chemical Products Co.; Creslan, an acrylic fiber, 3 types, American Cyanamid Corp.; Kodel, a polyester fiber, 6 types, Eastman Chemical Products Co.

1959 Agilon – Nylon filament for hosiery, Deering Millikin; Antron, nylon fabric, E.I. duPont de Nemours & Co.; Cadon, nylon resembling silk, Chemstrand Corp.; Celaperm, an acetate yarn, Celanese Fibers Co.; Coloray, viscose solution-dyed fiber, and Corval, cellulose fiber for blending with Orlon and wool, Courtald's North America Inc.; Colorspun, an acetate fiber, American Viscose Corp; Cupioni, cuprammonium yarns resembling silk dupioni, Beaunit Mills; Fortrel, a polyester fiber, Celanese Fibers Co.; Suracel, acetate fine twill lining fabric, Avondale Mills Inc.; Taslan, special process for making lightweight Dacron and nylon fibers, Branom & Co.; Zantel, rayon polynosic staple fiber, Hartford Fibers Co.; Zefran, modacrylic fiber for woven and knitted apparel, Dow Chemical Co.

Prominent Vintage Textile Mills, Converters, and Manufacturers

There are literally hundreds upon hundreds of American textile businesses which were or are part of the cloth industry over the past three centuries. As examples of a few methods of departure and survival, many mills were holding companies or names of buildings which were part of a mill complex, others were divisions, subsidiaries, alliances or co-ventures, yet others went bankrupt, while others simply closed their doors or were eclipsed, merged, folded in, sold and quickly closed or split among other textile companies or renamed. In many instances one sees the same backers on numerous mill ledger sheets.

To list them all is subject for another book and years of research. For many of the mills listed here, the manufacturing history is minimal due to sketchy information available. They are included, however, because of their products, contributions or reputation as a mill or manufacturer. Certain other mills and manufacturers have been omitted because of scarcity of or no available information or expired before our timeframe with no known later chronology available or weren't referenced by fabrics in this book. In some cases, a selling agent or distributor is listed in lieu of unknown mill or manufacturer as a means to connect fabric to a source. Companies listed here can be cross-referenced with fabric and finish brand names sections, pages 136 – 143.

Aberfoyle Mfg. Co. Inc., Chester, PA – 1889. Challies, crepes, flannels, fancy duck, ginghams, madras, japonette, print cloths, other wash goods, grenadine suisse, lustrous fabric, brilliant color, silk and cotton .

Algonquin Printing – See Columbia Print Works.

Allen Print Works, RI – 1830, as Phillip Allen & Sons, lightweight shirting and dress fabric prints; 1857, sold and renamed Woonsocket Company Print Works; 1871, incorporated as Allen Print Works.

American Bleached Goods Co. – See Ponemah Mills.

American Fibre Chamois Co. – Fibre Chamois waterproofed interlining for skirts, puffed sleeves, flared skirts.

American Hair Cloth Co., Pawtucket, RI – Hair Cloth crinoline interlining with pure hair filling.

American Print Works, Fall River, MA – 1835. Selling agency established in 1910. Textile involvement started by Bordon family when William Bordon began producing duck bolts made of hemp in 1722; 1868, renamed American Printing (Cotton Mills Division) after a fire; owned Fall River Iron Works Co. for weaving cloth; 1909, made Dolly Madison percales for Sears, APC wash fabrics; 1930, plant moved to Tennessee. See M.C.D. Bordon & Sons.

American Viscose Corporation (AVISCO) – 1930 – 1989. Country's largest producer of viscose rayon and staple, later acetate, polyester and polypropylene; renowned for such brands as Crown, Crown-tested, AVISCO, Colorspun, Petalspun; 1963, sold to FMC; 1972, sold to AVTEX Synthetic Fibers; 1982, never fully recovered from textile recession, and in 1989, closed all operations and declared bankruptcy.

Amoskeag Cotton & Woolen Manufactory, Manchester, NH – 1831, sold and renamed Amoskeag Mfg. Co. At peak of operations, had sixty-four mills covering a mile and a half of ground and housing 700,000 spindles and 23,000 looms which turned out 500,000 yards of cloth each week. Famous for Daisy Cloth, Romper Cloth, rayon, cotton chambrays, crash, denims, ginghams, sheeting, flannels and dobbies. 1935, bankrupt; reorganized as Amosekag Industries representing eighty different business. At time of bankruptcy it was the largest textile manufacturer in the world.

Androscoggin Mills, Lewiston, MA – 1860. Rayon crepes, fancies, bedding, Ripplette.

Arnold Print Works, North Adams, MA – 1811, known as Adams North Village Cotton Manufacturing Co.; 1862, sold and changed to Harvey Arnold & Co.; 1876, reorganized as Arnold Print Works; latter 1870s new owner operators changed name to North Adams Print Works; 1985, out of business. Bleach, dye and finish on print rayons and cottons, superfine organdies, silks, mohair luster. Produced fabric for Cohama and Waverly and La Bell Crepon diagonal patterns.

Bancroft, Joseph & Sons – Everglaze chintz, Staze-Rite Banlon, and Bancare. Marquisettes and organdies. Acquired William Simpson & Son. 1962, sold to Indian Head Mills Inc.

Barnes, Sumner & Putnam, Worcester, MA – Cashmere Imperial black silks.

Beldings Bros. & Co., NYC – Dress silks and linings, pure-dye satins, name woven in selvage.

Edwin E. Berliner & Co., NYC – Woven pieced goods of cotton, rayon, wool Aralac and flax fibers. Alltyme and Alltyme Crepe among trademarks.

Arthur Bier & Co., NYC – ABC Fabrics printed on every selvage.

Boott Mills, Lowell, MA – 1834. 1905, reorganized; 1953, sold to Overseas Development Corp.; 1955, sold to Northern Textile; 1956, mill and property shut down and sold. Voiles, drills, twills, towels, oxford cloth. "Boott Mills" stamped on every yard of selvage.

M.C.D. Bordon & Sons, NY – 1910. Selling agent. Cotton printed, and dyed piece goods. Advertised itself in the 1930s as largest manufacturer of figured cotton dress materials in the world. See American Print Works.

William H. Brown, Son & Co., NYC – Kindergarten Cloth, pieced goods of cotton, wool and mixed cotton and wool.

Bunting-Jenkin, Kreer & Co., NYC – Argentine Cloth.

Burlington Mills, NC – 1923, renamed Burlington Industries. Leading manufacturer of wool worsted and worsted-blend fabrics, denim, cotton and cotton-blend fabrics and waterproof synthetics for the apparel market; and woven jacquard mattress ticking and jacquard interior furnishing fabrics. 1945, acquired Postex; 1960s, acquired Ely Walker; 2001, filed for Ch. 11; 2003, W. L. Ross & Co. new owner; 2004, combined with Cone Mills; renamed ITG (International Textile Group).

Burton Bros & Co., NYC – Dress goods, Burton Fabrics, fast-dye wash fabrics.

Fred Butterfield & Co. Inc, NYC – Heatherbloom cotton taffeta; Sell and Repent cotton, woolen and silk piece goods.

Cheney Bros., Mount Nebo Silk Co, Manchester, CT – 1838. 1843, name changed to Cheney Bros.; silk manufacturers. Luxurious brocades, silks, Crepe Meteor®, pioneered in waste-silk spinning method and the Grant's reel. By 1880s, was one of the nation's largest and most profitable silk mills. 1923, fortunes declined due to industry-wide overproduction and competition from new fibers such as rayon.; 1955, purchased by J.P. Stevens & Sons for liquidation; sold to Gerli Incorporated of New York.; 1978, mills and surrounding neighborhood declared a National Historical Landmark District; 1984, mill permanently closed. Most of the mill buildings sold to developers for converting into luxury apartments and offices. Also see J.P. Stevens.

H. B. Clafins Inc., NYC – Most likely a distributor or selling agent. Bontex wash fabrics, Kiddie Cloth, cotton and silk piece goods, Gilberta linings and piece goods.

Cocheco Manufacturing Company, Dover, NH – 1812, as Dover Cotton Factory for printed cottons; also known as Dover Manufactory Co; 1863, Cocheco Woolen Mill, then Cocheco Manufacturing Co.; 1909, sold to Pacific Mills, became the Cocheco Division. 1955, division folded with sale to Lowenstein & Sons. Famous for its novelty and dress prints. See Pacific Mills.

Cohn-Hall-Marx, NYC – Tubrite cotton, acetate, rayon and silk.

Columbia Print Works, Fall River, MA – Prints and percales. See Algonquin Printing.

Cone Mills Export & Commission Co., NYC – 1891, sellers of textile goods produced in southern mills. Early 1900s, built its own manufacturing plant in Greensboro, NC called Proximity Mfg. due to its closeness to cotton fields. Became world's largest denim maker and a supplier for Levi Strauss. 1948, reorganized as Cone Mills Corp.; 1950s, became international; 2003, filed bankruptcy, bought by W.L. Ross & Co.; 2004, combined with Burlington Industries; renamed ITG (International Textiles Group).

Concordia – Gallia Corp. – 1929. Concordia Silk Mills Div., Philadelphia PA; ribbons and broad silks, rayon, ribbon loom, dye, bleach.

Concordia Mfg. Co., Valley Falls, RI – Concordia Gros de Paris, rayon and silk yarns.

Cranston Print Works Co., Cranston, RI – 1920. Early 1800s Sprague Print Works; post-Civil War sold to B.B. Knight which operated plant as Fruit of the Loom; 1920, sold to Consolidated Textiles and reorganized as Cranston Print Works; 1936, purchased one of the earliest Slater mills in Webster (Oxford) MA; 1949, acquired a plant in Fletcher NC; 1987, became employee-owned. Also see Slater and B.B. & R. Knight.

Crompton-Richmond Co., NYC – Corduroy, velveteen; Cravenetted finish; oldest and largest manufacturer of corduroy and velveteen in the country.

Dan River Power and Manufacturing Company, Danville, VA – 1882. 1909, renamed The Riverside and Dan River Cotton Mills, Inc.; 1964, changed to Dan River Mills, Inc.; 1970, renamed Dan River Inc.; famous for its ginghams and high-quality woven cotton and cotton blend fabrics for apparel and men's dress shirting fabrics and Wrinklshed brand name; 1997, acquired the assets of The New Cherokee Corporation, leading producer of light-weight yard-dyed woven fabrics in the Western Hemisphere; 1998, acquired The Bibb Company; 2000, acquired Import Specialist Inc.; 2003, filed for Chapter 11 and as of this printing has emerged and is under reorganization.

Duplan Silk Corp., NYC – Baronette sports silk and broad silk piece goods.

Eddystone Mfg. Co. – Also known as Simpson Print Works and, Eddystone Print Works. 1895, Wm Simpson founder, Philadelphia PA.. Dye, finish, mercerize, nap, Brandenburg print percales and other print cottons; Eddystone Simpson cottons featured in 1895 – 1896 *Montgomery Ward* catalog and mourning and dress prints in 1897 *Sears & Roebuck* catalog; 1955, sold to Indian Head Mills Inc.

Ely & Walker, Ely & Walker Dry Goods, St. Louis, MO – 1870. Firm founded by David Walker who through marriage into the Bush family would become the great-great and great-great-great-grandfather of two United States presidents. 1911, acquired Quadriga Cloth Co., and Postex Cotton Mills 1945. Quadriga Cloth Co. made or sold Quaker Chintz prints. Quadriga Cloth was needleized between 1932 – 1938. Also sold Gilbrae Fabrics, cotton, wool, silk, rayon, silk goods, and knitted goods. 1955, sold Postex to Burlington which listed E&W as Member of Burlington Industries from 1960s to 1980s.

N. Erlinger, Blumgart & Co. Inc., NYC – Everfast, cotton, silk, linen, mixed piece goods.

Foreman Fabrics Inc., NYC – Rayon, cotton, silk and blends.

The Forstmann Company, Victor Forstmann Inc. – Internationally famous for its wools. 1904, Forstmann Woolen Co.; 1947, bought by J.P. Stevens and relocated to Dublin Woolen Mill GA, part of the M.T. Stevens division; 1986, Stevens spun off all wool operations; plant renamed Forstmann & Co.; 1999, Victor Woolens Products purchased plants and brand name; renamed Victor Forstmann Company. Also see Pepperell, J.P. Stevens, WestPoint.

Fracon Mills, NYC – Persian lawn, nainsook and Swisses.

Franklin Mfg. Co., Baltimore, MD – Moneyworth fabrics, cotton piece goods, Moneyworth Ironclad dress galatea and Ironclad khaki.

Fruit of the Loom – See B.B. & R. Knight.

Gilbert Mfg. Co., 514-516 Broadway, NYC – Fast black sateen, linings, Pres de Soie and Radium silks, Flaxon combed lawn, organdies, dimities, mousselines and mulls.

Henry Glass & Co., NYC – Possibly selling agent; Peter Pan Fabrics, Tinkerbelle Fabrics; Polly Prim, cotton goods; rayon crepe introduced in 1931 – 1932. Peter Pan now owned by Marcus Bros.

S(imon) H(enry) Greene & Sons, Riverpoint, RI – Manufacturers of Washington and Martha Washington Prints. 1830s established Clyde Bleachery and Print Works. Produced prints of all kinds; famous for indigoes and turkey red prints. One of many mills forced to close in 1920s during the Scituate Reservoir project (RI). Not known at this point if this is the S. H. Greene which merged with McCrory chain in 1929.

Guilford Mills, Greensboro, NC – 1947, began with two tricot knitting machines; 1965, joined Cluett Peabody to form Oak Ridge Textiles; 1978, bought Beauknit Mills to obtain lycra; 2001, filed for Ch. 11; 2002, reorganized to focus on selected apparel businesses and automotive and technical textiles; 2004, sold to Cerebus Capital Mgt, will continue same operations.

Harlomoor Co., NYC – Linnette, chased-finished duck.

Hamilton Manufacturing Co., Lowell, MA – 1828. Produced calicoes and dress prints.

Harris Tweed Association, Lewis-Harris Island, Outer Hebrides, Scotland – Firm is the largest maker of the unique Harris Tweed fabric with a 95 percent share of the market, employs about 200 islanders to hand weave, spin, dye and finish wool at home before returning it to mills where it is washed, marked and sent to buyers under the Harris Tweed signature. 1840s, hand-loomed production began; 1909, Association formed; 1934, regulations relaxed to allow weavers to use factory-spun as well as hand-spun wool; 1937, Harris trade-mark patented; 1976, rejected bid to convert to electric looms; 2002, up for sale as owner neared retirement with no successor to take over his business. Turkish firm currently among the leading bidders for the company.

Havens and Geddes Co., Indianapolis, IN – Quaker Lady dress goods, piece goods, sheeting, curtains, chamois-finished longcloth for fine underwear.

Helwig Silk Dyeing Company 1903, Philadelphia, PA – Began in 1876 as Erler & Helwig; 1882, Helwig & Spiers; 1884, Albert Helwig & Co. Famed for its German and Swiss dyeing techniques which owners brought with them from Europe and for continued experimentation in skein dyeing. In 1900, Helwig was one of the first to use the tin weighting process developed in Germany in 1887, which combined tetrachloride of tin with tungstate of soda. Also one of the first to use newly developed Swiss ribbon looms. As business increased, dye plant moved to nearby Wissinoming on the Delaware River in 1914 for sufficient water supply. Products included specialty dyeing of floss and spun silks for upholstery, ribbon and millinery trades, first manually then converting to latest technology in equipment enabling fastness and later washability and stretching to increase luster. With advent of the three types of rayon, latest equipment was added in 1920s for dyeing that fiber. At that time Helwig began specializing in the revolutionary dyeing of silk goods in the piece. 1962, company dissolved.

Wm. Hollins & Co., Ltd, UK – Clydella Viyella, wool, and cloth goods. Later became Viyella Ltd. 1970s, sold to Coats chain; 2002, put on auction block; 2003, sold to Birmingham Group.

Hope Manufactory Co.,Salmon Hole, RI – 1806. Former Hope Furnace Co. estab. 1765. 1800, sold at auction, converted to cotton spinning mill; 1820, power looms introduced; 1821, all equipment sold to Ephraim Talbot; 1844, sold again and merged with Lonsdale Mills; 1847, incorporated as the Hope Company; 1899, Lonsdale built the Ann and Hope Mill. It is unclear whether that event pertained to the joint names Hope Lonsdale Mills which appears on labels in that era.

House of Lowenstein – 1898. See M. Lowenstein & Sons.

Indian Head Mills, Indian Head Mills Inc., Indian Head Inc. – 1953 – 1975. 1953, Indian Head Mills Division separates from Textron to form new company. Pursued increased finished goods and cloth production and acquisition program for converters and end-users. 1955, acquired Naumkeag Steam Cotton Co.(Pequot Mills); 1957, acquired J.L. Stifel and Sons; 1961, acquired Jos. Bancroft & Sons (Banlon) and Wm. Simpson and Wm. Skinner &

Sons; 1970, sold Indian Head Finished Goods Division to Springs Industries; 1975, Indian Head Inc. folded into Thyssen-Bornemisza; 1982, Thyssen sold division to Hansen Industries; 1994, Hansen demerged and reorganized as US Industries Inc. See Jackson Mills, Nashua Mfg. Co., Textron Inc., J.L. Stifel, Skinner and Springs Industries.

Ingram Interlining Co., NYC – Cheveret interlining.

Jackson Mills, Nashua, NH – 1830, Birthplace of Indian Head fabric. 1830 acquired a defunct company called Indian Head Mills; 1830 renamed Jackson Mills, continued to manufacture a fabric called Indian Head; 1916 acquired by Nashua Mfg. Co. See Nashua, Textron, Indian Head.

Johnson-Cowden-Emmerich Inc., NYC – Cinderella, satin two tones.

Johnson Mfg. Co., NYC – Sea Island colorfast zephyrs, bicycle logo.

King Phillip Mills, NYC – Cambric, lawns, nainsooks, printed batistes.

B.B.& R. Knight, Providence, RI – 1852 – 1920. 1889, purchased Lippitt Mills; 1887, Fruit of the Loom created; 1920, sold to Consolidated Textiles and reorganized as Cranston Print Works. Burlington Industries current owner. Alpine Rose (name stamped in selvage) sheetings, muslins, corset cloth, cambric, fine cotton goods, sateens, book cloth, dobbies, prints, starchless lawns, voile, batiste. Also see Cranston Print Works and Slater Mills.

Lancaster Mills, Clinton, MA – Kalburnie gingham, cotton goods.

Liberty of London, UK – 1874. Famous for its fine merchandise and superior quality imported fabrics, mostly from the Orient. Then branched out to purchase woven grey goods and engaged UK dyers, finishers and designers to produce the finest fabrics on the market. 1884, established the Paris store Maison Liberty which closed in 1932; 1890s, introduced Liberty Art Fabrics; 1904, purchased Merton Printworks and commissioned leading Art Nouveau artists to design fabrics; 1920s, introduced the small scale dainty floral Liberty prints, expanded line to all fine cottons including world renowned Tana lawn, silk, wool, and velvet; 1960, introduced the Lotus Collection of turn-of-the-century florals by famous designers; use of leading world designers continues to the present.

Lippitt Mills, West Warwick, RI – 1809-1889. 1889, sold to B.B. R Knight (Fruit of the Loom); 1920, sold to Consolidated Textiles; 1925, bankrupt, sold to Joseph Hayes; 1925, renamed Riverpoint Lace Works, still in operation.

M. Lowenstein & Sons, House of Lowenstein, Rock Hill, SC – 1899, fabric importers and jobbers of off-goods, grey goods production and end-user. 1938, printed the first rayon in the South. From 1940s through 1960s acquired Saratoga Victory Mills, Huntsville Mfg., Hamrick Mills, Limestone Mills, Lane Cotton Mills, Wamsutta Mills, Pacific Mills, Clark & Schwebel; 1970s, developed kettlecloth; 1985, merged with Springs Industries.

Lowell Weaving, Lowell, MA – Lotus Cloth, fine dress goods.

H.R. Mallinson & Co. Inc, NYC – Khaki Kool, pongee silk suiting; Pussy Willow, broad silk piece goods, printed and plain.

Manchester Mills, Manchester, NH – 1839, incorporated but not operational until 1845; 1847, reorganized as Merrimack Mills; 1851, renamed Manchester Print Works; 1874, renamed Manchester Mills. Produced cottons and wools.

Merrimack Mfg. Co., Lowell, MA and Huntsville, AL – 1822 – 1958. Corduroys, velvets, print clothes, Duckling Fleece. Merrimack prints featured in 1897 Sears catalog.

Milldale Textile Corp., Leonard, NY – Tommy Tucker, cotton piece goods.

Moygashel Ltd. Dungannon, Ireland – Linen operation for 1,500 years. Current operation is spinning, weaving and finishing linen cloth. 1953, Moygashel Ltd. formed by incorporating Stevenson & Sons Ltd and twenty-two other firms. 1969, acquired by Courtaulds, Ltd. Fabric only available as RTW.

Mt. Vernon Mills, Philadelphia – 1897. Madras, oxford cloth, cheviots, silk stripes, linen, grass lawn, silk on linen ground.

Nashua Mfg. Co., Nashua, NH – 1823. 1916, acquired Jackson Mills and Indian Head brand name; 1945, sold to Textron; 1953, sold to Indian Head Mills. Indian Head, Finesse percale with linen-like finish, Gilbrae ginghams, Parkhill ginghams, Lancaster Kalburnie ginghams, sheetings, blankets, dommets, flannels. See Jackson Mills, Indian Head Mills and Textron.

Naumkeag Steam Cotton Co., Salem, MA – 1839, operated Danvers Bleachery & Dye Works for bleaching, dyeing, finishing. Cotton goods, Pequot sheets. 1934, name changed to Pequot Mills; 1955, sold to Indian Head Mills. Also see Indian Head Mills.

Orinoka Mills – 1885. Sunfast fabrics and drapes.

Pacific Mills, Dover, NH; Mill in Columbia, SC – Largest manufacturer in world of cotton goods. Serpentine Crepe, a, crinkly surface cotton, Duretta, Pamico, Triam, cotton piece goods; 1955, sold to Lowenstein & Sons; 1985, became a division of Springs Industries through its Lowenstein purchase.

Pantasote Leather Co., Passaic, NJ – Dritex waterproof finish.

Parkhill Mfg., Fitchburg, MA – 1879-1928. Wash fabrics, Toile du Nord ribbon stripes and prints, Clitheroe zephyrs, 1mpress cords, fine zephyrs, corded novelties. See Nashua Mfg. Co.

Pepperell Mfg. Co. – Owner of Lewiston Bleachery ME & AL. 1845, named for Sir William Pepperell, whose former mill was on Pepperell site. Bleached and unbleached cotton piece goods, muslins, drills, jeans, toiles, Canton flannels, grey goods and moleskins. Griffin universally recognized logo. 1965, merged with Pepperell to form WestPoint Pepperell; 1993, acquired J.P. Stevens, renamed WestPoint Stevens. Also see Forstmann, Stevens and WestPoint.

Pequot Mills – Acquired by Indian Head Mills in 1955. See Naumkeag Steam Cotton Co.

The Pluette Company, Shaen Mfg. Co., NY – 1890s. Pluette waterproofing process for serge. Pluette stamped on back, 48" and 56" wide.

Polerized Fabrics Co., Taunton, NJ – Early 1900s. Sold dress goods direct from mill.

Ponemah Mills, Taftville, CN – 1867. See American Bleached Goods Co. Soisette, Flaxon, fine cottons, rayons, silks.

Pontiac Bleachery, Providence, RI – Hopewell brand textiles.

Priscilla Textile Co., NYC – Batiste, organdy and piqué.

Puritan Mills, Fayetteville, NC – Diana, fancy dress ginghams.

Queen Mfg. Co., NYC – Queen longcloth, silk, linens, cotton, worsteds.

Wm. F. Read, Philadelphia, PA – Landsdowne dress fabrics; Name stamped in selvage.

Relyea & Co., NYC – Relyea fabrics, white goods, linens and colored poplins.

Renfrew Mfg. Co., Adams, MA – Renfrew Fabrics, cotton piece goods, cotton wash goods, dress goods, shirting, tissue damasks.

Rigby Waterproof and Finishing Co., NYC – 1890. Finish and waterproof woolens; Fibre Chamois interlining.

Shepard, Norwell & Co., Boston – Fine wash dress, soft cashmere finish in rare colorings and beautiful patterns on ecru, cardinal, navy and black grounds; mourning effects, Empress jaconet lawn.

Simpson – See Eddystone.

Wm. Skinner & Sons, as Unquomonk Mills, Holyoke, MA – 1848. Braids, thread, silk and rayon goods. Renowned for its "Look for Name in Selvage" motto, quality bridal and lining fabrics and introduction of Ultrasuede in 1971. Other famous brand names include Barrister, Casino, Combat, Crepe Radiance, Esquire, Five Hundred Crepe line, Floriswah, King Cloth, Mellospun, Minaret, Rently, Soft-Sleep, Sunbak, Tackle Twill. 1961, purchased by Indian Head Mills; 1971, absorbed into Springs Industries through its acquisition of Indian Head. See Indian Head, Springs Industries.

S. Slater and Sons, Slater Mill, Pawtucket, RI – 1789, site of first successful water-powered cotton spinning factory in America; 1905, production ended at old mill, but continued at other newer mills; 1927, cornerstone from the original Slater Mill laid for the new Slater Plant located in South Carolina's upper Greenville County; 1933, the Old Slater Mill Association acquired the original building, restored to 1830 appearance, reopened as a museum in 1955; late 1930s, Slater Plant converted from cotton to rayon and acetate; 1936, one of the earliest mills sold to Cranston Print Works; 1946, J.P. Stevens & Co purchased Slater Plant as part of its Synthetics Fabric Division; converted it to weaving fiber glass in 1951; 1988, purchased by JPS Textiles, division of JPS Glass/JPS Industries. Also see Cranston Print Works, J.P. Stevens & Sons.

Sponge Cloth Mfg. Co., Lockport, NY – 1895. Sponge Crepon waterproofed stiffening and interlining.

Springs Mills, Springs Industries, Fort Mill, SC – 1887 – present. Manufacturer of ginghams and other quality fabrics and supplier of home furnishing lines and other diversified domestic lines. Famous brand names include Burlington House, Daisy Kingdom, Springmaid, Wamsutta. 1886 – 1887, LeRoy Springs & Co. and Ft. Mill Mfg. Co. were each founded and operated jointly by 1914; 1933, renamed Springs Cotton Mills, embarked on decades-long extensive acquisition program; 1945 – 1950s, Springmaid advertising campaign revolutionized ad industry; 1970, acquired Indian Head Finished Goods Division and Skinner brand name; 1982, renamed Springs Industries; 1985, acquired Lowenstein & Sons; 2003, honored by Textile World Magazine as Innovator of the Year.

J.P. Stevens & Co., as Stevens Woolen Mill, Andover, MA – 1813. Famous for woolens and flannels. 1947, purchased old Forstmann Woolen Mills; relocated operations to the Dublin GA plant which became

Dublin Woolen Mills in the M.T. Stevens & Sons Division; 1986, spun off Dublin plant and wool operations, renamed company Forstmann & Co.; 1993, acquired by WestPoint Pepperell to form WestPoint Stevens Co. Also see Cheney, Forstmann, Pepperell, West Point.

J.L. Stifel & Sons, Wheeling, WVA – 1835. Famous for its Indigo dyes and prints, drills, denim, calicoes, Miss Stifel Indigo Cloth, Bulldog twill shirtings; other brands include Bicycle, Express, Frosty Kool, Greytex, Ironclad, Menlo, Morocco, Perma-drape, Raintex, Shirtex, Sportador, Whirlwind. 1957, sold to Indian Head Mills. Permanent display of products are maintained at Stifel Fine Arts Center at the Oglebay Institute in Wheeling. Also see Indian Head Mills.

Textron Inc. – 1923 – present. 1923, founded as Special Yarns Corp., changing name to Atlantic Corp during WWII; 1945, name changed to Textron Inc., purchased Nashua Mfg. Co.; 1953, sold Indian Head Division which became a new company, Indian Head Mills; 1953 – present, Textron focuses on industrial and automotive market. See Nashua Mfg. Co. and Indian Head Mills.

Universal Mfg. Co., Woonsocket, RI – Cotton, silk in all designs, colors and models not found in ready-made garments.

Unquomonk Mills – 1848. See Wm. Skinner & Sons.

Wamsutta Mills, New Bedford, MA – 1847. Sheetings, pillowcases, oxfords, percales, lingerie cloths, lawns, fancies, cambric, nainsook, longcloth, poplins, yacht duck, high-grade yarns, bleached cotton. 1954 sold to Lowenstein & Sons; 1985, became a division of Springs Industries through its Lowenstein purchase.

Warren Featherbone Co., Three Oaks, WI – 1883. Featherboning, bias tape, braid, rickrack and other notions. 1995, relocated to Gainesville GA. Changed production to children's and infant apparel and swimwear. Company observed 121st anniversary, 1995.

Waycraft Mills, Cambridge, MA – Jerray all-wool jersey; sold knits, rayons direct from mill.

Weil Fabric Co., Philadelphia, PA – Silk, wool, and cotton.

WestPoint Mfg. Co., West Point, GA – Acquired Chattahoochee Mfg. Co. following Civil War, cloth sheetings, drills and piece goods; 1965, merged with Pepperell to form WestPoint Pepperell; 1993, acquired J.P. Stevens, renamed WestPoint Stevens. 2004, declared bankruptcy; 2005 sold to investor group W. L. Ross & Co., LLC. Also see Forstmann, Pepperell, Stevens.

T.D. Whitney & Co., Boston, MA – Mandalay tissue, a dress cotton in stripes, plaids, plains.

Windsor Print Works Co., North Adams, MA – 1828. 1843, sold and leased to Arnold & Jackson; 1860, sold and renamed Richardson, Freeman & Co., then W.W. Freeman & Co. 1874, renamed Freeman Mfg. Co.; 1891, incorporate as Windsor Co.

𝔗extiles 𝔄re 𝔄 𝔚oven 𝔓art of 𝔄merican 𝔥istory

The journey of clothmaking from field to our closet is shown here in a collective pictorial representative of the various stages of textile production.

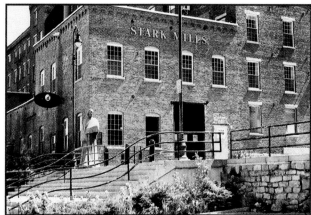

Living history: Two of the country's earliest mills now offer tours. Boott Mills in Lowell, MA and Stark Mill, one of 20 plants in the Amoskeag complex, Manchester, NH. Photos courtesy James Cummings.

Another just recently closed mill with a long and prestigious history is Lancaster Cotton Mills Mill, built in 1895 and later renamed the Lancaster Plant when it became part of the Spring Cotton Mills. Some of its huge structure is shown in a view from the spinning room by artist George Erban, late 1940s. Courtesy White Homestead Archives/Springs Industries. See mill histories section.

THE LANCASTER PLANT of THE SPRINGS COTTON MILLS

Painted by George Erban

Modern cotton harvesting followed by super gin machinery which can clean and compress as many as sixty 500-lb. bales an hour. Shown here is a new bale coming off the press following ginning. Courtesy National Cotton Council of America.

After sheep shearing, fleece is thrown to skirting table to remove inferior wool and other matter. Courtesy American Sheep Industry Association Inc.

Bundles of flax, after retting or soaking, are stood upright and dried again, then put through rollers to crush the straw, separating soft flax fibers from harsh straw. Belgium, mid-1960s. Courtesy *Masters of Linen*.

Hanks of combed flax pass through a drawing machine to emerge in a continuous wide ribbon called a sliver. This repetitious operation draws the flax thinner until all small fibers lie parallel, ready for spinning. Belgium mid-1960s. Courtesy *Masters of Linen*.

Another drawing operation – 1940s roving room where cotton slivers are drawn into thread and placed on bobbins in preparation for spinning. Courtesy White Homestead Archives/Springs Industries.

1939 spinning room. Spindles operating at 12,000 revolutions per minute draw threads to final fineness in preparation for weaving. Courtesy White Homestead Archives/Springs Industries.

Today's high-tech spinning machines increase production as much as sixty pounds per man-hour. Courtesy Georgia Textile Manufacturers' Association.

Silk operations at the Hellwig Silk Dye Co., Wissinoming, PA, in the weighting and skein color dyeing sections. Early 1900s. See mill histories. Walter Stock collection.

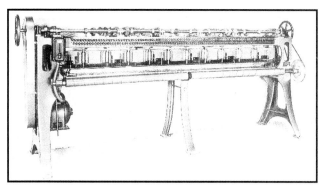

Hand looms provided cloth for home and played an important part in early textile manufacturing as a cottage industry for many early mills. From *Trades and Occupations* by Carol Belanger Grafton. Courtesy Dover Publications.

The 1930s produced the first tufting machine which was adapted from a single-needle commercial Singer sewing machine so that it would tuft thick yarn on unbleached muslin without tearing fabric. In the 1940s it would be adapted for carpet production. Courtesy Georgia Textile Manufacturers' Association.

The modern weave room features computerized state-of-the-art equipment. Courtesy Georgia Textile Manufacturers' Association.

1941 inspection room where cloth was examined and graded. Today, computers monitor quality during every stage of production. Courtesy Georgia Textile Manufacturers Association.

Cloth for consumption, from *Trades and Occupations* by Carol Belanger Grafton. Courtesy Dover Publications.

Cloth journey's end – models of perfection soon to be clothed in a myriad of fabrics as shown in *Standard Garment Cutting*, 1897, and *Trades and Occupations*, by Carol Belanger Grafton. Courtesy Dover Publications.

Bibliography

Books:

Adams, Bolton, and Irwin. *Drygoodsman's Handy Dictionary*. The Drygoodsman, ST. Louis. 1912.

Affleck, Diane L. Fagan. *Just New from the Mills: Printed Cottons in America Late Nineteenth and Early Twentieth Centuries*. North Andover, Mass.: University Publishing Association, 1987.

Angelo, Bonnie. *First Mothers: The Women Who Shaped the Presidents*. New York: Perennial, 2001.

Bendure, Zelma and Gladys Bendure - Pfeiffer. *America's Fabrics*. New York: Macmillan, 1947.

Bennett, Frank P. *A Cotton Fabrics Glossary*. Boston, New York, etc.: Frank P. Bennett & Co., Inc.; C. 1914.

Burnham, Dorothy K. *Warp and Weft: A Textile Terminology*. Toronto: Royal Ontario Museum, 1980.

Carmichael, W. L., George Edward Linton, and Isaac Price. *Callaway Textile Dictionary*. LaGrange, GA: Callaway Mills, 1947.

Cole, George. *Dictionary of Dry Goods*. W. B. Conkey Co. 1892.

Denny, Grace G. *Fabrics and How to Know Them*. Philadelphia, London: J.B.Lippincott Company, 1923, 1927, 1928, 1936, 1942, 1953, 1962.

Eisinger, Larry. *The Complete Book of Sewing*. New York: Greystone Press, 1972.

Emery, Irene. *The Primary Structures of fabrics: An Illustrated Classification*. Washington, D.C.: Textile Museum, 1980.

Hardingham, Martin, Mary Anne Sanders, and Fiona Roxburgh. *The Fabric Catalog*. New York: Pocket Books, 1978.

Hollen, Norman R. and Jane Saddler. *Textiles*. New York: Macmillan, 1968.

Hoye, John. *Staple Cotton Fabrics: Names, Descriptions, Finishes, and Uses of Unbleached, Converted, and Mill-finished Fabrics*. New York and London: McGraw-Hill Book Co., 1942.

Humphries, Mary. *Fabric Glossary*, 2nd ed. Upper Saddle River, N.J.: Prentice Hall, 1999.

_____. *Fabric Reference*, 3rd ed. Upper Saddle River, N.J. : Pearson/Prentice Hall, 2004.

Joseph, Marjorie L. *Introductory Textile Science*. New York: Holt, Rinehart, and Winston, 1972.

Lepson, E., *Ashort History of Wool and Manufacturing*, 1953.

Linton, George Edward. *The Modern Textile and Apparel Dictionary*. Plainfield, N.J.: Textile Book Service, 1973.

Newcomb, Ellsworth and Hugh Kenny. *Miracle Fabrics*. New York: Putnam, 1957.

Nichols, Henry Wyman William H Broomhead. *Standard Cotton Cloths and Their Construction*. Fall River, Mass.: Dover Press, 1927.

Perry, Walton. *The Story of Textiles: A Bird's-eye View of the History of the Beginning and the Growth of the Industry by which Mankind is Clothed*. Boston, Mass.: J.S. Lawrence, 1912.

Potter, Maurice David and Bernard P. Corbman. *Textiles: Fiber to Fabric*. New York: Gregg Division, McGraw-Hill. 1967.

Tortora, Phyllis G. and Robert S. Merkel. *Fairchild's Dictionary of Textiles*. 7th ed. New York: Fairchild Publications, 1996.

Woolman, Mary Schenck and Ellen Beers McGowan. *Textiles: A Handbook for the Student and the Consumer*. New York: MacMillan, 1926.

Catalogs:

Bellas Hess. New York City: National Cloak and Suit Co. 1909, 1922-1923.

Charles Williams Stores, Inc. Catalogue. New York, NY: Charles Williams Stores, Inc. 1927.

Chicago Mail Order Company Catalogue. Chicago, IL: Chicago Mail Order Company. 1930 and 1934.

Montgomery Ward Catalog. Montgomery Ward Co.1887, 1925, 1939-1940, 1941, 1948, 1950, 1951, 1952, 1961.

National Bellas Hess. New York City: National Cloak and Suit Co. 1937,1939, 1946-1947, 1952.

Sears & Roebuck Catalogue. Chicago, IL: Sears, Roebuck, & Co. 1897, 1902, 1908, 1920, 1928, 1933, 1942, 1943.

Internet Sources:

avtexfibers.com

danriver.com

1911Encyclopedia.com

Fabrics.net

jpsglass.com

Liberty.co.uk/company.

quickpics.com

Take Our Word.com

Vertestable.com. Sixteenth century and seventeenth century Tailoring Terms.

virginia.edu/history. Textile Glossary from Eighteenth century Virginia Runaway Projectwise.

Magazines:

Elite Styles. October 1913. Elite Styles Co. N.Y.

Farm & Home. October, 1922. Phelps Publishing Co., Springfield, MA.

Ladie's Home Journal. Curtis Publishing Co., Philadelphia 1890, 1894, 1895, 1896.

McCall's. November 1904. The McCall Co., N.Y.

Modern Priscilla. July, 1910. Modern Priscilla Co., Boston.

Munsey Magazine. 1908. Frank A.Munsey, N.Y.

Peterson's Magazine. 1863. Charles J. Peterson, Philadelphia.

Pictorial Review. New York: The Pictorial Revue Co. May 1914.

Workbasket. November 1948. Modern Handcraft Inc., Kansas.

Miscellaneous Periodicals/Sources:

Cotton: From Field to Fabric. National Cotton Council, NY. 1951.

History of Wool. American Wool Council. 1968. Wool Education Center, American Wool Council and The Wool Bureau, Denver.

Rayon Glossary: Definitions of Rayon Fabrics and Terms Used in Connection with Rayon. American Viscose Corporation, NY. 1950.

Sheldon's Weekly Dry Goods Price List. New York, NY: Sheldon's Weekly Dry Goods Co. August 24, 1871.

Walter Stock and Pennsylvania Department of State and the Free Library of Philadelphia.

Wright's Sewing Booklet No. 21, 1929. WM.E.Wright & Sons, Orange NJ.

Wright's Sewing Booklet No. 26, 1932. WM. E. Wright & Sons, Orange NJ.

GLASSWARE & POTTERY

4929	**American Art Pottery**, 1880 – 1950, Sigafoose	$24.95
5907	Collector's Encyclopedia of **Depression Glass**, 15th Ed., Florence	$19.95
5748	Collector's Encyclopedia of **Fiesta**, 9th Ed., Huxford	$24.95
5609	Collector's Encyclopedia of **Limoges Porcelain**, 3rd Ed., Gaston	$29.95
1358	Collector's Encyclopedia of **McCoy Pottery**, Huxford	$19.95
5677	Collector's Encyclopedia of **Niloak**, 2nd Edition, Gifford	$29.95
5678	Collector's Encyclopedia of **Nippon Porcelain**, 6th Series, Van Patten	$29.95
5618	Collector's Encyclopedia of **Rosemeade Pottery**, Dommel	$24.95
5842	Collector's Encyclopedia of **Roseville Pottery**, Vol. 2, Huxford/Nickel	$24.95
5921	Collector's Encyclopedia of **Stangl Artware**, Lamps, and Birds, Runge	$29.95
5680	Collector's Guide to **Feather Edge Ware**, McAllister	$19.95
6124	Collector's Guide to **Made In Japan Ceramics**, Book IV, White	$24.95
1523	Colors in **Cambridge Glass**, National Cambridge Society	$19.95
4714	**Czechoslovakian Glass** and Collectibles, Book II, Barta	$16.95
5528	Early American **Pattern Glass**, Metz	$17.95
5257	**Fenton Art Glass** Patterns, 1939 – 1980, Whitmyer	$29.95
5261	**Fostoria Tableware**, 1924 – 1943, Long/Seate	$24.95
5899	**Glass & Ceramic Baskets**, White	$19.95
6127	The **Glass Candlestick** Book, Vol. 1, Akro Agate to Fenton, Felt/Stoer	$24.95
5840	**Heisey Glass**, 1896 – 1957, Bredehoft	$24.95
6135	**North Carolina Art Pottery**, 1900 – 1960, James/Leftwich	$24.95
5691	**Post86 Fiesta**, Identification & Value Guide, Racheter	$19.95
6037	**Rookwood Pottery**, Nicholson/Thomas	$24.95
5924	**Zanesville Stoneware** Company, Rans, Ralston & Russell	$24.95

DOLLS, FIGURES & TEDDY BEARS

2079	**Barbie** Doll Fashion, Volume I, Eames	$24.95
3957	**Barbie** Exclusives, Rana	$18.95
6022	The **Barbie** Doll Years, 5th Edition, Olds	$19.95
3810	**Chatty Cathy** Dolls, Lewis	$15.95
4559	Collectible **Action Figures**, 2nd Ed., Manos	$17.95
6134	Ency. of Bisque **Nancy Ann** Storybook Dolls, 1936 – 1947, Pardee/Robertson	$29.95
4863	Collector's Encyclopedia of **Vogue Dolls**, Stover/Izen	$29.95
5904	Collector's Guide to **Celebrity Dolls**, Spurgeon	$24.95
1799	**Effanbee Dolls**, Smith	$19.95
5611	**Madame Alexander** Store Exclusives & Limited Editions, Crowsey	$24.95
5689	**Nippon Dolls** & Playthings, Van Patten/Lau	$29.95
5253	Story of **Barbie**, 2nd Ed., Westenhouser	$24.95
1513	**Teddy Bears & Steiff** Animals, Mandel	$9.95
1808	Wonder of **Barbie**, Manos	$9.95
1430	World of **Barbie** Dolls, Manos	$9.95
4880	World of **Raggedy Ann** Collectibles, Avery	$24.95

JEWELRY, HATPINS, & PURSES

1748	Antique **Purses**, Revised Second Ed., Holiner	$19.95
4850	Collectible **Costume Jewelry**, Simonds	$24.95
5675	Collectible **Silver Jewelry**, Rezazadeh	$24.95
3722	Collector's Ency. of **Compacts**, Carryalls & Face Powder Boxes, Mueller	$24.95
4940	**Costume Jewelry**, A Practical Handbook & Value Guide, Rezazadeh	$24.95
5812	Fifty Years of Collectible Fashion **Jewelry**, 1925-1975, Baker	$24.95
1424	**Hatpins** & Hatpin Holders, Baker	$9.95
5695	**Ladies' Vintage Accessories**, Bruton	$24.95
1181	100 Years of Collectible **Jewelry**, 1850 – 1950, Baker	$9.95
6232	**Plastic Jewelry** of the 20th Century, Baker	$24.95
6039	Signed Beauties of **Costume Jewelry**, Brown	$24.95
4850	Unsigned Beauties of **Costume Jewelry**, Brown	$24.95
5696	Vintage & Vogue Ladies' **Compacts**, 2nd Edition, Gerson	$29.95
5923	**Vintage Jewelry** for Investment & Casual Wear, Edeen	$24.95

FURNITURE

3716	American **Oak** Furniture, Book II, McNerney	$12.95
1118	Antique **Oak** Furniture, Hill	$7.95
3720	Collector's Encyclopedia of **American** Furniture, Vol. III, Swedberg	$24.95
5359	Early **American** Furniture, Obbard	$12.95
3906	**Heywood-Wakefield** Modern Furniture, Rouland	$18.95
1885	**Victorian** Furniture, Our American Heritage, McNerney	$9.95
3829	**Victorian** Furniture, Our American Heritage, Book II, McNerney	$9.95

INDIANS, GUNS, KNIVES, TOOLS, PRIMITIVES

1868	Antique **Tools**, Our American Heritage, McNerney	$9.95
1426	**Arrowheads** & Projectile Points, Hothem	$7.95
6021	**Arrowheads** of the Central Great Plains, Fox	$19.95
5616	Big Book of **Pocket Knives**, Stewart	$19.95
5685	**Indian Artifacts** of the Midwest, Book IV, Hothem	$19.95
5826	**Indian Axes** & Related Stone Artifacts, 2nd Edition, Hothem	$19.95
6130	**Indian Trade Relics**, Hothem	$29.95
6132	Modern **Guns**, Identification & Values, 14th Ed., Quertermous	$14.95
2164	**Primitives**, Our American Heritage, McNerney	$9.95
1759	**Primitives**, Our American Heritage, Series II, McNerney	$14.95
6031	Standard **Knife** Collector's Guide, 4th Ed., Ritchie & Stewart	$14.95

PAPER COLLECTIBLES & BOOKS

4633	Big Little Books, A Collector's Reference & Value Guide, Jacobs	$18.95
5902	**Boys' & Girls' Book** Series, Jones	$19.95
4710	Collector's Guide to **Children's Books**, Vol. I, Jones	$18.95
5153	Collector's Guide to **Children's Books**, Vol. II, Jones	$19.95
1441	Collector's Guide to **Post Cards**, Wood	$9.95
2081	Guide to Collecting **Cookbooks**, Allen	$14.95
2080	Price Guide to **Cookbooks & Recipe Leaflets**, Dickinson	$9.95
4733	**Whitman Juvenile Books**, Brown	$17.95

TOYS & MARBLES

2333	Antique & Collectible **Marbles**, 3rd Ed., Grist	$9.95
5681	Collector's Guide to **Lunchboxes**, White	$19.95
4566	Collector's Guide to **Tootsietoys**, 2nd Ed., Richter	$19.95
4945	**G-Men and FBI Toys**, Whitworth	$18.95
5593	Grist's Big Book of **Marbles**, 2nd Ed.	$24.95
3970	Grist's Machine-Made & Contemporary **Marbles**, 2nd Ed.	$9.95
6128	**Hot Wheels**, The Ultimate Redline Guide, 1968 – 1977, Clark/Wicker	$24.95
5267	**Matchbox Toys**, 3rd Ed., 1947 to 1998, Johnson	$19.95
5830	**McDonald's** Collectibles, Henriques/DuVall	$24.95
5673	Modern **Candy Containers** & Novelties, Brush/Miller	$19.95
1540	Modern **Toys** 1930–1980, Baker	$19.95
5920	Schroeder's Collectible **Toys**, Antique to Modern Price Guide, 8th Ed.	$17.95
6140	**Teddy Bear** Treasury, Vol. II, Yenke	$24.95
5908	**Toy Car** Collector's Guide, Johnson	$19.95

OTHER COLLECTIBLES

5898	Antique & Contemporary **Advertising Memorabilia**, Summers	$24.95
5814	Antique **Brass & Copper** Collectibles, Gaston	$24.95
1880	Antique **Iron**, McNerney	$9.95
3872	Antique **Tins**, Dodge	$24.95
5607	Antiquing and Collecting on the **Internet**, Parry	$12.95
1128	**Bottle** Pricing Guide, 3rd Ed., Cleveland	$7.95
3718	Collectible **Aluminum**, Grist	$16.95
5676	Collectible **Souvenir Spoons**, Book II, Bednersh	$29.95
5666	Collector's Encyclopedia of **Granite Ware**, Book II, Greguire	$29.95
4857	Collector's Guide to **Art Deco**, 2nd Ed., Gaston	$17.95
5906	Collector's Guide to **Creek Chub Lures** & Collectibles, 2nd Ed., Smith	$29.95
3966	Collector's Guide to **Inkwells**, Identification & Values, Badders	$18.95
3881	Collector's Guide to **Novelty Radios**, Bunis/Breed	$18.95
4864	Collector's Guide to **Wallace Nutting Pictures**, Ivankovich	$18.95
5929	Commercial **Fish Decoys**, Baron	$29.95
5683	**Fishing Lure Collectibles**, Vol. 1, Murphy/Edmisten	$29.95
6141	**Fishing Lure Collectibles**, Vol. 2, Murphy	$29.95
5911	**Flea Market Trader**, 13th Ed., Huxford	$9.95
5262	**Fountain Pens**, Erano	$24.95
6227	**Garage Sale** & Flea Market Annual, 11th Edition, Huxford	$19.95
3819	**General Store** Collectibles, Wilson	$24.95
2216	**Kitchen Antiques**, 1790–1940, McNerney	$14.95
5686	**Lighting Fixtures** of the Depression Era, Book I, Thomas	$24.95
5603	19th Century **Fishing Lures**, Carter	$29.95
5835	**Racing Collectibles**	$19.95
2026	**Railroad** Collectibles, 4th Ed., Baker	$14.95
5619	**Roy Rogers and Dale Evans** Toys & Memorabilia, Coyle	$24.95
1632	**Salt & Pepper Shakers**, Guarnaccia	$9.95
5091	**Salt & Pepper Shakers** II, Guarnaccia	$18.95
3443	**Salt & Pepper Shakers** IV, Guarnaccia	$18.95
6137	**Schroeder's Antiques** Price Guide, 21st Edition 2003	$14.95
5007	**Silverplated Flatware**, Revised 4th Edition, Hagan	$18.95
6239	**Star Wars** Super Collector's Wish Book, 2nd Ed., Carlton	$29.95
3977	Value Guide to **Gas Station Memorabilia**, Summers	$24.95
4877	Vintage **Bar Ware**, Visakay	$24.95
5925	The Vintage Era of **Golf Club** Collectibles, John	$29.95
4935	The W.F. Cody **Buffalo Bill** Collector's Guide with Values, Wojtowicz	$24.95

This is only a partial listing of the books on antiques that are available from Collector Books. All books are well illustrated and contain current values. Most of these books are available from your local bookseller, antique dealer, or public library. If you are unable to locate certain titles in your area, you may order by mail from **COLLECTOR BOOKS**, P.O. Box 3009, Paducah, KY 42002-3009. Customers with Visa, Master Card, or Discover may phone in orders from 7:00–5:00 CT, Monday–Friday, Toll Free **1-800-626-5420**, or online at **www.collectorbooks.com**. Add $3.00 for postage for the first book ordered and 50¢ for each additional book. Include item number, title, and price when ordering. Allow 14 to 21 days for delivery.

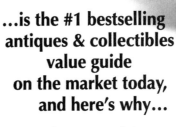